Giving MY PAIN a VOICE
A Path to Healing

ANNI B. JOHNSON

Copyright © 2017 by Anni B. Johnson

All rights reserved. No part of this publication may be reproduced, stored in a retrieval system, or transmitted, in any form or in any means – by electronic, mechanical, photocopying, recording or otherwise – without prior written permission.

Events, locations, and conversations have been based solely on the authors recollection. All names and identifying details have been changed to protect the privacy of individuals.

ISBN-10: 0-9986580-0-6
ISBN-13: 978-0-9986580-0-1
Library of Congress Control Number: 2017902028

Cover Designer: Panagiotis Lampridis
Book Interior Design and Layout: Sarco Press

To my husband, for the value he places on family, and the fight it took to keep us connected. I am forever grateful to God for gifting you to me and me to you. We are what love is made of, and an example of how hard marriage is and what it requires to be successful. I love you, babe.

To my daughter, for always knowing who she is and not allowing others to deter her from what she knows to be true for herself, even if that means standing alone. I am in awe of your courage every day.

To my son, for having the tenacity and wherewithal to live life as he sees fit despite the world around him. Keep pushing, and never let anyone steal the joy that lives within you.

I dedicate this book to everyone who has the courage to take off their mask and look at themselves authentically in order to stand firm on a foundation that will equip them to live the life they seek.

Chapter 1

As I exited the Grand Central Parkway onto Northern Blvd, I sat in the morning rush hour traffic in route to the worst job in my career. As usual, I was dreading going to work and facing the relentless frustration and stress of an environment that was so hostile I referred to it as Satan's Den. When I was offered the position, I knew I didn't want the job, and my gut feelings were screaming for me to turn it down. After discussing the job with my family, the enticement of "name your own price" was too much temptation, and I grudgingly accepted the position. I had compromised myself once again by doing something I knew was not right for me, and I was paying the price. I was knowingly walking into hell each day, and I still showed up.

As my car inched toward the next traffic light, I turned up the radio to distract myself from my misery. A song I had never heard before began to play and caught my attention. The tune was reminiscent of old school R&B, and I loved the slow tempo. I turned up the volume as the words started.

I need your forgiveness
And your mercy too
I must be all kinda crazy
For what I've done to you
I hope you understand
That my heart is true
Mistakes, I've made em
But I'm making a change for you.

Tears began to roll down my face as I listened. For some strange reason, I usually only pay attention to the beat of most songs, but the words of this song were speaking to a place much deeper within. As Tyrese Gibson's song, *Shame,* played on, visions of my life flashed before me. I felt pain that I'd been unknowingly carrying for sixteen years, the burden that had been sitting on my weakened shoulders. In that moment, I felt broken. Shattered, lost and not understanding the flood of emotions that were overcoming me. "What in the world is going on?" I asked myself.

As I continued to drive, I made a right turn onto 111th and crossed Astoria Blvd. *I'm tired. Just so tired of everything.* I felt like driving far away from everything and everyone, under no circumstances to return to the likes of this life that never felt like my own anyway. Instead, I drove straight to Satan's Den, as I did every day, and I sat in the parking lot, trying to wrap my head around my thoughts.

Although these feelings caught me totally off guard on this day, deep down, I had been plagued with some struggles for a long time. I wiped my tears, grabbed my purse, and prayed for strength to fight off the evil from this crazy, demonic job. I took a deep breath, exhaled and exited the car. For whatever reason, it took this song, this job, and this moment for me to finally wake up to the fact that something much bigger was going on in my soul and in my life. I was unhappy. Feelings of discontent bubbled to the surface as I recognized the wretchedness of my daily existence, including my unfulfilling career.

For many years I had questioned, *Whose life is this?* In no way, shape or form could I have ever imagined *this* being my life.

I should have been happy, right? Respectably married by the age of 27, I had a handsome husband, two beautiful children - a boy and a girl, a lovely home, a six-figure salary, and a dog. My flexible work schedule allowed me to come and go as I pleased, and I made enough money that I didn't have to think twice about purchasing anything I wanted. By most societal standards, I was living the American dream. I had everything I've ever wanted. Then why did I feel so miserable? *I'm not happy!* There, I said it. God forbid I admit it out loud for anyone to hear, because even saying it to myself made me feel guilty. But why? Isn't it every human's desire to be happy?

On my long ride home riddled with tons of traffic, I called my closest friend, Emily, who always put things into perspective for me. She and I had been friends since 1995 when we both worked for an adoption agency in New York City. I told her about the flood of emotions I had experienced, and she was as blunt as I expected.

"When are you going to tell yourself the truth?" she asked.

"The truth?" I innocently replied.

Emily told me that over the years I have changed from the feisty, confident, goal-oriented, no-holds barred woman she had known me to be. Once I got married and had my first child, Emily believed something happened that changed the course of my life. I pretty much laughed at that notion, because I could never understand why she would always think that. You see, Emily seems to have some form of psychic talent. In her tell-it-like-it-is approach, she's able to see things that are not always obvious. It's as if God blessed her with the ability to connect with people in ways that help them view things through a different lens. Isn't that what we all need? To be able to change our perspective on what we *think* we see or know? Emily reminded me again of her theory that something had happened to change me and pointed out that I have been carrying a lot of burdens for a while; some mine and some others, and my struggle in navigating through it has finally reached its breaking point.

I was groomed by my parents to be the "responsible" one, and it has always been natural for me to take on leadership roles within my family and the work place. You want a problem solved - I'm your girl! I will help from beginning to end and follow up to make sure everything is working out well. I accept challenges provided I know I can handle them. The Superwoman mentality, with my red cape flying in the wind, is what I know. It's a custom fit. I am your crime-fighter, your advocate, your healer, your comforter, your tear wiper, your mediator and then some. I juggle it all, keeping the balls in the air and my feet firmly planted, because I'm no failure. I am perfection at its best! I reminded Emily of this fact.

In true Emily fashion, she said, "Oh really now? So, Superwoman, why are you struggling? Perfection doesn't struggle, does it?"

Yeah. Why am I struggling? I didn't dare acknowledge any truth in her question.

"Take a good honest look at where you are," Emily said. "There is something that is causing you to feel the way that you do, and it's not because you are Superwoman."

Food for thought. I thanked her, as I always do before hanging up the phone. I spent the next few months thinking about what she said and began to evaluate my life.

Things aren't always as they seem. The physical existence I portrayed on the outside didn't match the emotions I experienced on the inside. There may be some truth to what Emily had said. I have questioned for years: *Is this my life? It sure doesn't seem that way.* Sometimes I would share this thought with my husband, Dalton, but it always caused conflict. He interpreted it to mean I didn't want to be with him. I didn't completely understand it myself, so I did a poor job at convincing him that he was wrong. I never quite connected to the life I was living.

I always felt like I was living outside of myself and watching a stranger's life unfold. I guess I had to admit that something was off. Why couldn't I feel connected to this life? "Take an honest look," my friend advised. My thoughts were immediately drawn back to a period of time right before my wedding.

Chapter 2

As I searched my heart in silence, my thoughts returned to December of 1998 and January of 1999. This was approximately three months before my wedding. The events that led up to my wedding date should have been the happiest of my life. In retrospect, they were dreadful, filled with red flags and the gut feelings I had ignored that were now coming back to haunt me.

Dalton and I met in February of 1993 while I was a senior in college. I was out on a date at Garden City Lanes with a guy I had met earlier in the day. He and I were assigned to Lane One, and Dalton and his group of friends were in Lane Two. Mind you, the entire bowling alley was practically empty, and as my date and I approached Lane One, I thought, *Out of all the open lanes, they stick us next to these guys!* Being naturally shy, I didn't focus much on Lane Two and don't recall noticing Dalton, as there were so many people with him. My date and I bowled two games and then we went to shoot pool near the concession area.

Dalton later told me that as we walked away he told his best friend, Ryan, that he was going to marry me.

Ryan asked, "Do you know her?"

"No," Dalton replied, but he was very confident I was going to be his wife.

Seven days later, my friends and I had gone to a local nightclub we enjoyed. As we entered, we checked our coats, and proceeded downstairs towards the lounge. As we were about to enter the main doors of the dance floor, someone tapped me on the shoulder. I turned and there was this big, muscular guy in a tan leather jacket saying, "Remember me?"

Being a no-nonsense person I quickly quipped, "No!" and started to walk away. I was never known to be the most sociable person, and I could be a bit rude when approached by men in clubs, just to make things perfectly clear that I wasn't interested.

Before I could get away, the well-built guy said, "You were at the bowling alley last Saturday with a real corny guy, and I was in the lane next to you. I'm Dalton."

"Oh, ok," I replied as my friends pushed through the main doors to the dance floor, leaving me behind. "I'm Anni."

We engaged in small talk and exchanged some flirty sarcasm before I entered the club, leaving Dalton in the lounge area. "Nice to meet you," I said as I turned away and pushed through the doors.

A few hours later, my friends and I were leaving for the night, and Dalton was still in the lounge where I had left him. He asked for my phone number and if we could take a picture together before I left. You see, back in the day, clubs had a photographer with a Polaroid camera taking pictures for $5. It was out of character for me to say yes to such a request, considering Dalton was a total stranger, but I agreed. I gave Dalton my number, and as we walked out, my friends asked, "What are you going to do with that big grown man?"

The next day, Dalton called me. The more we talked, the more we enjoyed each other's company. He shared with me what he had told Ryan that night at the bowling alley. I found it strange, because how could anyone know whom he or she was going to marry in an instant? I didn't believe in love at first sight, and honestly, I thought he was a bit crazy.

Dalton and I dated exclusively for one year. My family liked him, and unbeknownst to me, he and my brother had known each other for years. Dalton had been to my house several times, he'd gone on trips with my brother, and they were part of the same circle of friends. The fact that I lived on campus was probably the reason we never crossed paths during those encounters with my brother. I fell madly in love with Dalton over the course of our first year together. I had only dated one other guy before Dalton, but Dalton was different. He was special, and he made me feel special.

Dalton was the type of person who would do anything for me. He would do whatever he could to make me happy, comfortable, or bring joy into my day. He was that guy your friends would measure their boyfriends against. I was proud of our relationship, as no one had ever made me feel so special. I felt like the center of his world and my heart was bursting with happiness.

Chapter 3

After a year of courtship, Dalton called and asked to come over to see me. I remember the day perfectly. I had returned home from work and I was exhausted. I spent most of my day in the field visiting foster families, and traveling on and off the subway and buses. I said, "Sure. Come on over."

Dalton didn't sound like his usual self. He had a slight heaviness in his voice, something different that I couldn't put my finger on. Being oblivious, I didn't put much thought into it and waited for him to get to my house. At the time, I was living with my parents and my brother, and they had become accustomed to Dalton coming and going, although not too late. My dad was (and still is) very old school and did not want to see anyone in his house after midnight.

I peeked out the window and saw Dalton pulling up in his dark blue Volkswagen Jetta that always smelled like pancake syrup for some reason. My heart fluttered a little because even after a year I was still getting butterflies every time I saw him. Most people in my life would be surprised to hear that, since I usually had a tough exterior. I opened the door before he even rang the bell. "Hey there," I said with a big smile on my face.

"Hi," he said with less enthusiasm.

"What's wrong?" I asked as he entered.

"Nothing much," he said with no expression on his face. *That's strange.* This was the first time I had seen this somber side of him.

"What's going on with you?" I asked in an inquisitive fashion.

"I need to talk to you," he said.

"Ok. Shoot. What's up?" I replied.

"I think it's time we had some space," he said abruptly. My heart sank and the butterflies disappeared.

"Excuse me," I said with a puzzled look plastered all over my face. "You want *what*?"

"I want to be honest with you and tell you the truth. I've decided I want to explore other options," he admitted.

"Other options?" I said, trying not to scream. "What other options?" Refusing to go into further detail, Dalton said he wanted to take a break from our relationship. "Why?" I asked in an angry tone.

"I just need to," he said sheepishly.

"So you're interested in someone else, huh?" I said vindictively.

"Possibly," he finally admitted.

"Get out! Get out now!" I shouted. Before he could even get out the front door, I slammed it.

My mind was racing, and I wondered how my Mr. Perfect could do this to me. I had opened my heart to him, unlike any other relationship before. Whether it was a boyfriend or one of my other friends, no one had permission to examine my full heart. I'd always kept it well protected. It had layers of bubble wrap to keep it from being bumped or bruised, not to mention the amount of bricks that shielded it from any potential injury. I had unwrapped it with love and purposefully handed it to

Dalton on the finest china. And what did he do? He threw my heart on the ground, plate and all, and left it there, as broken as the shattered porcelain. How could I have let this happen? Instead of tears, I was full of rage. I swallowed the pain and indignation, and the embarrassment of being dumped. I vowed never to allow myself to be in that situation again.

I got up the next morning and called out sick. I was too tired and drained from not getting any sleep as I replayed the breakup in my mind all night. After my mother and brother left for work, I called my friend, Marcia, who heard the stress in my voice as she listened intently to what had happened.

"I'm coming over right now," she said. Before I could say no, she hung up, and it wasn't long before Marcia was at my door.

"What did this bastard do?" she demanded to know as she entered the house.

I broke down and started to cry.

"What? Why you crying?" Marcia was surprised by my breakdown. She, nor any of my other friends, had ever seen me cry. I was the stoic non-emotional friend. Nothing ever fazed me, or if it did, I never showed it. My emotions always came out as either anger or revenge. Never tears. Marcia was flustered as she tried to comprehend what she was witnessing.

"You gonna let him get you to tears?" she asked.

"I loved him. He was different," I pleaded.

Marcia admitted to being shocked and confused herself. "Listen, at least he told you. Guys don't usually do that," she said.

"Yeah, I know, but it doesn't make it feel better," I admitted.

"Would you rather he not tell you?" she replied.

When I thought about it, so many guys would never tell the truth about wanting to see someone else. They would just do it and hope they aren't caught. Actually, I wasn't too sure they would even have a conscience to be truthful in the first place. So should I be happy he told me? Was this Dalton's misguided way of protecting me? It still didn't feel right and I was mad, regardless of his intentions.

Marcia said, "At least he was honest. You have to give him that. That's kind of unheard of." Marcia and I laughed as we reminisced about my last boyfriend who outright cheated, tried to hide it, and still got caught. And he had the nerve to deny it even though he was caught with the side chick in his car. Lessons learned in the "game of love" I suppose. I couldn't help feeling that I didn't deserve this, but who does?

Six months passed and I was back in the full swing of dating and hanging out with friends. I hadn't talked to Dalton at all during this time. He never called me, and I didn't reach out to him. We didn't roll in the same circles, so maintaining our distance was easy. I started dating a friend I knew from high school and was having a good time. We spent a lot of time together, but our relationship started to become strained. He felt we were ready for intimacy, and I thought otherwise. One day at his house, we had a huge argument about it, and he cursed me, which I would not tolerate. Quite like anyone else in my life who does me wrong, I cut him off. No one was going to pressure me into something I was not ready to do. As I pulled away from that relationship, Dalton called.

"Yeah?" I answered.

"Hello. How are you?" Dalton said.

"I'm good," I said calmly. You know we always have to sound like we are "living the life" when an ex calls.

"Can we talk?" he asked.

"Um, about what?" I asked sarcastically. The last time we talked, he was making his exit, so what exactly would he have to say? "I'm not interested in talking. Besides, you said all you needed to say six months ago."

"I made a mistake," Dalton said humbly. "I want you back."

Oh, really now, I was thinking. "Ok...," I said inquisitively. "Well, I'm not an object. You don't get something back because you want it. Besides, you don't deserve someone like me. Stay with whomever you thought was better."

Obviously, he had thought someone was better than I was. Was she prettier? What did she do that I didn't? I started to wonder about the questions one would think I would have wanted to know six months ago. Why does he want to get back together? Did she dump him and he wanted to come crawling back because he was lonely? Could I trust him?

That's the problem with us women. Men treat us like dirt and we accept them back into our lives despite the hurt and pain they caused us. *Don't I think higher of myself than to get back with a person who dumped me? Aren't I worthy of better?* So many thoughts were running through my mind that I was confusing myself, but I agreed to meet with Dalton despite the many questions that had no real answers.

When we met, he approached me with humility in his voice and the admission of his guilt. "I was wrong. I know I hurt you, and I'm sorry," he started. "I made a mistake and I'm asking for your forgiveness," he added.

"Why should I give you another chance?" I asked.

"I'm human and I made a mistake and I love you," he said with a serious look on his face.

"You love me?" I asked. "Love is not supposed to hurt, but you hurt me." I started to remember the humiliation and heartache Dalton caused on the night that he told me he wanted to explore his options.

"I know," he said shamefully.

"Why now? Why are you here? What happened?" I inquired.

"You're supposed to be my wife, remember?" he asked.

"Remember? You sure as hell didn't treat me like I was supposed to be your wife," I said angrily.

"I want to start over. A fresh start," Dalton said.

"Well, I'm currently seeing someone," I answered dismissively.

15

"So, drop him. He's probably corny like the last guy anyway," he said with a teasing smile.

Smiling back, I said, "No. No, he's not corny." Well, he wasn't corny but I was definitely not interested in seeing him after our last argument. "We'll see, but I'm not making any promises."

Why do men think that it's that easy to change their minds, and believe we will jump right in line? Dalton had stripped me of my trust. Once you lose that, it's hard to regain it, if ever. This is where women go wrong. We are too forgiving. We lower our standards and accept the behavior that goes against what we believe is true for our own well-being. Where do we learn that? Our mothers, or maybe from our fathers in the way they treat our mothers. We're definitely mimicking familiar behavior. But the real question is, are we even aware of it?

My choice to go back with Dalton or not had everything to do with my mother's choices and the kind of relationships I witnessed as a child. Ultimately, I chose to take Dalton back, but was it the right decision? Only time would tell.

Chapter 4

Over the next few years, Dalton worked diligently to regain my trust. He returned to the caring man who did everything he could to make me happy. In February of 1998, five years after we first met, we became engaged. Although our love grew stronger and stronger with each passing year, I started to notice the struggle Dalton was having as he attempted to keep me happy and manage the drama in his own life.

You see, Dalton had become a father when he was twenty-two years old, about two years before we met. He was dependent on his family to assist him in caring for his son, Christopher. Although Dalton's liaison with Christopher's mother was brief, she had always been in the picture and had a close-knit relationship with Dalton's family. Early on, it was obvious that Christopher was being used as a means to disrupt my relationship with Dalton. During our courtship, Dalton and I had done everything we could do to incorporate Christopher into our life as a couple. Despite our best efforts, Dalton proved to be no match for his mother, Mrs. Johnson, his Aunt Agnes, and Christopher's mother. The three of them always seemed to have an agenda to work together to form a wedge in my relationship with Dalton and Christopher.

Dalton was patient in bringing me around Christopher and waited for the right time to introduce the two of us. After about four years into our relationship, when Christopher was six years old, we took him on vacations to North Carolina, amusement parks, and local attractions. I even taught Christopher how to ride his bike. In our world, Dalton and I were working together to bring his son into our lives respectfully and purposefully. I had been around Dalton's family and had interacted with Christopher's mother on many occasions prior to our engagement. Despite it all, the women in Dalton's family did not respect our union. As in many families where the parents are no longer together, they made Dalton feel guilty and tried to convince him that Christopher and I could not both exist in his life.

The disrespect was especially evident during the traditional Thanksgiving and Christmas dinners where I had to play musical chairs since I wasn't allowed to sit in certain seats. "No, you can't sit there because Mrs. Johnson sits there, and Rachel sits next to her, and Lauren sits next to Rachel," they would say. I realized in those moments that I was not welcome. But why? I had never done anything to any of them. I have been just as my parents raised me - kind, considerate, compassionate, and respectful.

Dalton turned a blind eye to the mistreatment and as a result of our silence and complacency, we were pushed to the far end of the table, sometimes behind guests that weren't even family. Dalton and I felt invisible within his family. Why would Dalton not say anything? Why wouldn't he stand up for me, for us? I'm sure the fact that they were instrumental in helping him raise Christopher had a lot to do with it. Well, that's the excuse I made for the disrespect I felt when I was around them. I get it. They thought they were protecting Christopher. But from what? Couldn't they see I meant him no harm?

Dalton and I had dated for five years, and I thought I had proved myself to Dalton's family. After all this time it was as if they expected me to never accept Dalton's son as a part of my life. I felt as if I wasn't worthy to be in their presence. I'd never given them any reason to doubt my love for Dalton or Christopher. Why wasn't I good enough for them? I was a young woman with a good head on my shoulders. I had conducted my life in the standards by which most parents compare their children. I was an Ivy League graduate, earning my master's degree at the age of 23, working full time, paying my own bills, and I had no children. Maybe they were used to women in Dalton's life who were in stark contrast to what I brought to the table.

Despite never understanding the reasons for his family's behavior, I endured their abuse for most of our courtship and well into our marriage. When you marry someone, you lose sight of the influence his or her family can exert. Extended families can make or break a marriage, especially when the signs are so evident early on. What makes us ignore the signs? Love? Disbelief that the family could actually drive a wedge between two people who love each other? Families are powerful dynamics, and they can cause some real destruction in a marriage. Were Dalton and I strong enough as a unit to withstand the daggers and passive aggressive undertones, especially when it came to Christopher being a part of our lives? Christopher was a child, but in his family's eyes he could do no wrong, and they used him to exclude me, which forever divided us. It was made perfectly clear that I wasn't wanted and my feelings didn't matter.

The weight of trying to please everyone had taken a toll on Dalton. He had been accepted into a prestigious training program and was undergoing the training and studying that ensued. Dalton did his best at trying to fit his son and me into his limited free time. However, Dalton's family guilted him into spending "quality time" alone with Christopher. They thought

I was a distraction and felt it wasn't fair for Christopher to have me around when he was spending time with his dad. It hurt to be excluded from an essential part of Dalton's life, but being mature about the situation, I understood.

During any time that Dalton had to spend with me, he was always called home for something. There would be times when Dalton was out with me and he would receive a call asking him to come put his son to bed. The stress was getting to him as he tried to juggle everything. We started to fight with one another about the control his family had over him. Dalton's baggage had started to become visible to me, and I could not understand why he was controlled by his family so easily. Mrs. Johnson would say, "I'll fix you," whenever Dalton attempted to go against her demands.

I'll never forget the struggle I was having when I had to write a mock suicide letter for one of my graduate courses. I told Dalton about it, and he had one written in a split second. That's when I knew there was something much deeper going on with him. The pressure and responsibility of his family and the constant requests from his friends to help with things happening in their lives was taking an emotional toll on him.

As the contents of Dalton's baggage became more evident, other struggles seem to pull on his psychological strings. Being an adoptee carried a tremendous weight that he had been dragging around for decades. The discovery that he had been adopted and the lack of connection to his adoptive family had not escaped him. The knowledge of being adopted had ignited a quest beyond measure as Dalton's fantasies replaced what he thought was true. Fantasies about who his birth parents were, what they looked like, where they come from, and if he had a big family. The unsettling compulsion to seek out and find his birth parents took up residence and found a daunting spot within the baggage of Dalton's life. My employment at an adoption agency didn't help.

My work as a Social Worker in the Birth Parent Department

brought up an enormous amount of emotional turmoil for Dalton. He started to ask questions, become angry, and felt lost. He had an incredible hole in his soul that was becoming more and more prevalent. We started talking openly about his adoption, his feelings, and the disconnect he felt from the Johnsons. He was yearning for unconditional love, and he always felt his mother's love was only given with strings attached. When he didn't meet Mrs. Johnson's demands, her vindictive response was "I'll fix him" rather than showing she loved her child. Unfortunately, Mr. Johnson, Dalton's adoptive father, was like most men in those days, who left child rearing to the mothers. Mr. Johnson is a gentle soul, but he gave Dalton the same thing his father gave him. No emotions. No quality time. No interference with his wife's decisions.

Dalton loved me and I loved him, but Dalton's love for me was intense. It was almost as if I was his blood supply, being pumped through every vein, every artery, traveling at high rates of speed through his heart, to his brain, and the entire infrastructure of his being. I meant more to him than anybody else in is life. Realizing how much he depended on me, I began to shoulder Dalton's burdens. Isn't that what I was supposed to do? Women have mimicked their ability to carry their men's problems for years, often to their own demise. Why was I going to be different?

Chapter 5

I grabbed Dalton's baggage and jumped right in it with him. Like cleaning out a messy closet, I sorted through Dalton's burdens, attempting to discard the unnecessary and salvage the useable. Sifting things around, trying to organize his pain and shuffle his hurts. Throwing things out of that bag wasn't easy, as Dalton loved to hold onto things that were familiar. Changing established patterns was difficult, especially since I was an outsider, and his friends were asking, "Where did this girl come from?"

After I dealt with Dalton's baggage, I emerged in a new role. I became Dalton's mother. A mother who protected her child at all cost. A mother who loved unconditionally. A mother who was comforting, a listener, and a mother who would make everything better. Dalton was dependent on me to play this role, since he never had anyone who fit the mold of his definition of a mother, anyone who loved him unconditionally or had the ability to take care of him, instead of him taking care of everything and everybody.

Mrs. Johnson cared for him, and he is forever grateful for her and Mr. Johnson. To this day, he credits them for giving him a life he probably would not have had if he had not been adopted. Nevertheless, there's something about a mother's unconditional love, and he did not get this from Mrs. Johnson. I had become what he wanted and needed.

We were too young and immature to recognize the role I played as well as the significance later on, but I took the reins willingly, seeing that my past dictated that I had to. As was demonstrated to me as a child by my mother, I was in agreement to change who I was supposed to be for Dalton into who he needed me to be for his well-being. It was a classic example of the generational patterns that often continue throughout families as we unknowingly are cast to play certain individual roles. Shouldering Dalton's dysfunction was how I had been cast.

After our engagement and the implementation of our new roles as a mother figure with a son who needed unconditional love, Dalton and I found comfort. Dalton's family and friends weren't quite sure what was going on, but they noticed that they were unable to command the same amount of control and attention they had used in the past.

Christopher's mother, Mrs. Johnson, and Agnes had a slight upper hand, as some women like to use kids as pawns to control the chessboard. As any good father would admit, Christopher was Dalton's weakness, and rightfully so. He did everything possible to avoid disputes and place his son in the middle of the tug of war. Despite our efforts, Dalton's family was successful in driving a wedge smack down the middle of Dalton's life.

During the year of our engagement, Dalton moved into an apartment in upstate New York with his best friend, Vaughn. After his graduation from the training institute, Dalton was assigned to work in Yonkers, and Westchester was a good place to be. It created distance from the people causing him the most stress, and being away from his family gave Dalton time to clear his head.

Although the division between Christopher and me had been waged early on in our courtship by Dalton's family, Dalton failed to make any attempt to bridge the gap that would be essential to successfully incorporating Christopher into our lives. I have to admit, however, finally having Dalton to myself felt good. We were no longer victims to the plots and schemes that were used to solidify the wedge that kept me from forming a healthy bond with Christopher. I too started to play a role in maintaining the gap since having Dalton's son removed from the equation seemed to make my life with Dalton easier. Distancing myself from Christopher meant I didn't have to deal with him or any of the women associated with him. Those three witches were ready to cast any harmful spell they deemed necessary to keep me out of their lives. I started to view Dalton as a separate entity, without Christopher, and I started building resentment as he represented a part of Dalton that didn't feel good to me as a result of other people's influences.

Christopher's presence always caused conflict in my relationship with Dalton, considering he allowed his family to dictate his actions. Dalton, his son and I would have been fine without every hand trying to stir the pot of our relationship. Sometimes it's best to let things be and play out with no interference. Egos and the power to manipulate can destroy even good intentions and cause life-long ramifications. The many attempts to drive me away were always in direct relationship to Christopher being Dalton's son and me not being welcomed into the family. Christopher had become the common denominator. My life with Dalton had come down to whether I could conform to being docile, which I refused to accept. As a result, Christopher's extension from Dalton became invisible to me. It was as if he no longer existed.

Chapter 6

Now that Dalton had moved to Westchester County and settled into his new place away from his family, we were finally able to focus on planning our wedding. Preparing for our wedding was an exciting and chaotic time. Picking seven bridesmaids and groomsmen and outlining the intricate details that go into a wedding of 260 guests can be nerve-racking, to say the least. I was happy. Happier than I had ever been. I had become successful at creating a space in my mind for Dalton's family and son. I knew I would eventually have to reach back in my memory and pull out some unpleasant thoughts while planning the wedding, but I refused to allow them to ruin my day.

The excitement of our upcoming wedding was felt from New York to North Carolina. My paternal grandmother, Bea, was even coming to my wedding. Unlike Mrs. Johnson and Agnes, I was deeply loved by my family. The woman Dalton's family believed me to be was far removed from the intelligent, kind, respected woman my relatives appreciated.

Dalton was heavily involved in the planning, sometimes too much, but it was important for him to play a role. This is a man who wanted his own engagement ring, and I gave him one. I was in love - what can I say? Dalton had a basic desire to be wanted, just as a woman receives that confirmation with a ring that represents hope and love. I found a gold ring with three rows of diamonds that extended from side-to-side that he could wear even after we exchanged wedding bands. Dalton was present at the bridal shower and helped host the event, although only one of his friends, Julian, and my brother were the only other men in attendance. It didn't take much to figure out they were there for the food and drinks! We had a great time celebrating our upcoming union with family and friends who loved us and supported our life together.

Life as we knew it was moving along nicely as we navigated our way through the complicated maze of our upcoming nuptials. Both Dalton and I commuted back and forth from Long Island and Westchester, daily sorting out the details of vendors, dresses, travel arrangements for guests, etc.

During one weekend, I went to see Dalton, and he seemed down, almost depressed. Vaughn was in and out of the apartment while I was there, but he also noticed that Dalton wasn't himself. We were riding on such a high with all the wedding planning, I couldn't understand why he was down. I must have asked Dalton a trillion times what was wrong, but he never gave a clear answer. I tried to cheer him up to no avail. I asked if he wanted me to go home so he could have time to himself and rest, but he declined. I didn't want to sit in "that" all weekend, now that I had way too much stuff to do besides sitting there and watching him sulk.

"Come on, Dalton, we've got things to do. We can't sit here and get nothing done," I pleaded.

"I don't feel that well," Dalton said. I asked if he wanted to go to the doctor, if he wanted soup, and anything else I could think of that would make him feel better. "No," he answered in a weakened voice.

Vaughn returned home, and he tried to get Dalton to talk

about what was going on with him. The more we pressed for answers, the more despondent he became. Vaughn and I are both Virgos, with little tolerance for emotional things, especially feelings we don't understand. As we continued to grill Dalton for an explanation for his behavior, Dalton started talking crazy, almost like in riddles.

Struggling to understand, Vaughn and I were baffled, but we attempted to comprehend what Dalton was saying. Was he losing his mind? What the hell is happening? Most of what Dalton was babbling was not in full sentences, and it was obvious he was in agony. Dalton fell to his knees and shouted, "I can't take it anymore!"

Vaughn and I were shocked because this seemed to come out of nowhere. We had been planning our wedding and enjoying the process along the way. "You can't take what?" I asked with my heart pounding. Before we knew what was happening, Dalton pulled out his work gun and put it to his head.

I started screaming, "What are you doing!? What are you doing?"

Vaughn disappeared, grabbed the phone and dialed 911. As I pleaded with Dalton to put down the gun, it seemed like hours before the doorbell rang. Vaughn told Dalton that he had called for help. Dalton went into panic mode as he stood up, placed his gun on the dresser, all the while asking Vaughn, "Why would you do that? Why would you call them? I can lose my job!" Vaughn said nothing in reply. He grabbed his keys, demanded I come with him and pulled me out the door. Vaughn ordered me to get into his car while Dalton calmly talked to the police officers who had been standing outside the front door.

Apparently, Dalton convinced the officers that it was a misunderstanding and they did not restrain him. Dalton ran over to Vaughn's car and begged me not to leave him. "Please don't leave me," Dalton pleaded repeatedly.

Vaughn, positioned in the driver's seat, looked at me and said, "Either get out or I'm driving off." The mother in me got out of the car, and I watched Vaughn drive away before I could even close the passenger door.

The officer asked me if I was all right. "Yes," I said, but I knew I wasn't. I was deathly afraid. Why did I get out of Vaughn's car? This was foreign territory. I'd been trained to handle incidents such as this, but I had never been directly involved with anything like this in my life. This was way out of my league, and I couldn't believe I was re-entering the apartment with a man in a troubled state of mind. What was wrong with me? Did I not value my life? I had no idea if I was going to be dead or alive by morning.

Well, I was alive, and I made it safely back to my parents' home. I never told anyone what had happened that day, and I don't recall ever discussing it with Vaughn. I have no idea if Dalton and Vaughn ever talked about it. It's been a skeleton in the closet for many years. I do know I experienced a level of fear I had never imagined, and you never forget something like that.

Chapter 7

A month after the incident with the gun, and three months before our wedding date, I spent the night at Dalton's apartment. Vaughn wasn't there, and it was only Dalton and me. I started to wonder if Vaughn purposely stayed away when I was there. I wouldn't blame him if he did, since Dalton had started showing signs of depression again. To say I was scared was an understatement, but the mother in me couldn't forsake him and leave him alone.

"Where's your work gun?" I asked when I got up the next morning. I awoke feeling anxious and thinking I probably should have asked Dalton about the gun the night before.

"It's locked in the safe," he admitted.

"What's wrong?" I said in a motherly voice. "What's troubling you?" Dalton started pacing, which made me nervous. "You're making me scared."

"Don't be. I will never hurt you," he said. As I watched Dalton pace back and forth, I knew something heavy was on his mind, but what was it? What was making him so miserable? He had started his new job; he moved; we were getting married. So what was the problem? Dalton sat me down on the edge of the bed in his bedroom. "I love you," he started.

"Yes, I know you do, but you're scaring me." I said as I stood up. "We really should get ourselves ready for work because we're both going to be late if we don't." I was attempting to divert his attention and get myself out of there.

He said, "Anni, please sit down. I have something to tell you." My antennae went up, and I was curious about what he had to say. *What do you have to tell me?* Dalton struggled to find the words, but the pain on his face was visible. *Was he dying?* I thought.

"Are you dying?" I asked.

"No. I'm not dying," he answered.

"What? What is it?" I demanded.

"I have to be truthful with you," he said quietly as he held his head low as if in shame. "I've been with someone else," he admitted.

"You what? Been with someone else? What does that mean exactly?" I asked.

"God told me I had to tell you. I can't get married without being honest with you," he stated.

"When did this happen?" I asked, as if the answer would make any difference.

"Last year," he admitted.

"Last year? And you're telling me now?" I asked. "Why? Why tell me three months before our wedding? Why didn't you come clean then?"

"I don't know. I don't know," he said. "I couldn't go through with marrying you carrying this burden. God convicted me to tell you, to be honest and truthful."

"Oh, you think you're getting married? Well, tell God thank you, but no thank you," I said with more anger than I thought possible. Dalton tried to set me down again, but I refused. At that point I didn't care if he killed me, himself or both of us, but I was not going to listen to anything else he had to say, and I definitely was not going to be sitting down to hear any more lies.

"You liar!" I shouted. "How could you do this to me? Better yet, how could I have allowed you to do this to me? I loved you. I believed in you when no one else did. I put it all on the line for you. I dishonored myself for you and this is how you repay me?"

"Please don't leave me. I need you," he pleaded. I grabbed the phone, called Mr. Johnson and told him to come and pick up his son because he was not well. During the phone call, I asked Mr. Johnson for a ride back to Long Island, and he agreed. While I waited for him to arrive, I packed my belongings that had been moved to the apartment. I kept silent as Dalton pleaded and begged me not to leave him.

Mrs. Johnson and Agnes had won. I give up. I couldn't marry this man. The list of reasons began in my head:

#1 – I fear him.
#2 – He's a cheater and a liar.
#3 – I can't trust him.
#4 – He's unstable.
#5 – His family hates me anyway.

These were issues no woman would *ever* want in a spouse. Why did he do this? Why couldn't he control himself? What is it about me that both of my boyfriends thought it was ok to cheat on me? One thing I knew for sure - I was not marrying Dalton no matter what!

Forty-five minutes later, Mr. and Mrs. Johnson arrived. Neither of them seemed shocked or overly concerned regarding Dalton's condition. I explained to Mr. Johnson what had happened as Mrs. Johnson stood in the corner, puffing on her cigarette with side eyes. *Who gave her permission to smoke in here anyway?* I wasn't going to tell her to take her cancer stick outside, and of course, Dalton was no match to confront his mother. She seemed unfazed as I briefly shed light on the situation. Both parents were emotionless as Dalton paced back and forth, pleading with me not to leave him. It was as if they didn't see him.

How could his parents not help their son as he was unraveling right in front of them? Why were they ignoring him, and not comforting him, as most parents would do? Mrs. Johnson was giving herself a tour of the apartment, and Mr. Johnson robotically stuffed random pieces of Dalton's clothing into a plastic bag. Dalton was a mess, as if he didn't know if he was coming or going. He tried unsuccessfully to get my attention, but I was numb to his pleas. "I'm not marrying you, so stop asking me," I snapped.

"Why? I told you the truth," he pleaded.

"I'm not marrying you," I repeated, with every word he uttered. Mr. Johnson tried to get Dalton to stop, but he was unable to handle the magnitude of what was happening. I would bet anything they had never seen Dalton in such a state. Exactly like Dalton's friends, his parents had probably never noticed the emotional side of him. He always portrayed strength. Physical strength.

Dalton was an immovable force, driven by the emotional turmoil he seemed to live on the inside. Mrs. Johnson's conditional love created a monster within him, on top of his issues about being adopted. I couldn't understand what was going on with Dalton anymore. He was self-destructing, and I wanted no part of him, ever!

The drive to Long Island was long and miserable as Dalton and I sat in the rear while his parents occupied the front seats. Mr. Johnson said absolutely nothing, but Mrs. Johnson attempted to make small talk. I was not interested in being phony and did not engage in her conversation, or interact with her crazy son, who continued to grab at my hand to hold it. As Mr. Johnson pulled up to my house, I jumped out, never uttering a word to any of them. Dalton rolled down the window and said, "I'll talk to you later, ok?"

I went inside the house and slammed the door shut. "You won't be talking to me," I said to myself. "You can go straight to hell where you belong."

Chapter 8

I got up the next morning exhausted. I hadn't slept all night as I tossed and turned in amazement at how my life was falling apart. I was set to marry the perfect man. The man I believed was kind, compassionate, honest and trustworthy. Looking back over our relationship, I couldn't pinpoint any red flags, with the exception of Dalton being honest with me about his interest in pursuing other dating options. Was that considered a red flag? I suppose to some it would have been. But what about his honesty in choosing to tell me that he wanted to date other people? Did he get brownie points for that? No. No, he did not. He broke up with me, and six months later, I took him back. Now, he confessed that he had been unfaithful an entire year earlier before deciding to be truthful. He was deceitful and dishonest. And he fooled me into believing he was different. He was like the rest, and I had been crazy to believe otherwise.

As I showered and got dressed for work, I felt angry. I had given this man all of me. Emotions unseen by most, were on full display for Dalton. Isn't that what women tend to do? We give men our hearts and souls, hoping they see us. Hoping they honor us. Hoping in return, they give us what we give them. We change and conform who we are to make them happy and content. But I didn't think I had to conform. We had a mutual give and take, and I believed we were happy.

As thoughts raced in and out of my mind, it was as if I had the devil on one shoulder and God on the other, and I was utterly confused. God wanted me to see the good in Dalton and hold on. But the devil? That joker told me he was no good. *He's absolutely like every man - a liar. Look at your father. Dalton's going to do you the same way your father does your mother. Do you want that in your life?* These questions and thoughts rang in my head the entire day. The wedding is off! I can't be like my mother. I can't and won't put up with that life of disrespect.

I called my matron of honor, Kameron, and my maid of honor, Marie. They have been my best friends since childhood, and I knew they would support my decision. I told them the wedding was off. They asked, "What? Why?"

"Can you believe he cheated on me? Me, of all people?" I asked angrily.

"What?" they both asked.

"When? With who?" Marie snapped.

"Last year sometime. I don't know with who. All I know is I'm not getting married," I said confidently.

"Oh, Lord. Are you sure?" Kameron asked.

"Most definitely," I said without hesitation.

Silence ensued as Kameron and Marie were searching their hearts to say something that would make it all better. But there was nothing that could be said to repair the shotgun blast that had blown my insides to pieces.

"Where do I go from here?" I asked them both in a defeated tone.

"You're going to pick yourself up, hold your head high and move forward," Marie said as Kameron agreed.

"Yeah! That's exactly what I'm going to do," I said in an attempt to convince myself of the ease in moving forward.

How does one move forward with ease? Do I get up and head back to work and skip my way through life? What about the gun, and Dalton's instability? How do I shake that off? I don't know, but I suppose I have no choice but to try to get past it.

"We'll take care of everything," Marie said.

The wedding invitations had already been mailed, and responses had started to come in. Vendors were calling to finalize details. Alterations had been scheduled, flights had been booked, and the travel agent was asking to complete payments and plans. The phone calls were overwhelming as I struggled to push them all back.

As the wedding date grew closer, I was being pressured by everyone in Dalton's circle to consider his state of mind. Seriously? Who was considering *my* state of mind? I hadn't told anyone in my family. Not my parents, my brother or anyone else in the wedding party, except Marie and Kameron. *I can handle this myself, like I handle everything else in my life.* But, Dalton's tight knit group was insisting I needed to help heal Dalton, forgive Dalton, stand by Dalton, and save Dalton. They could care less about how all of this was making me feel.

Dalton's mother called me one day and asked if I could come and see him. "He's in a lot of pain," she said.

Hell, so was I! In a weakened state, I agreed. I got in my car, and during the entire trip to Dalton's house I questioned my decision to see him. He had a whole village rooting for him. I stood alone in the attempt to fight through my pain and feelings of betrayal.

As I pulled up to Dalton's house and got out the car, a voice in my head said, *Go. Go ahead.* A different voice asked, *Are you stupid? Do you know what this man has done to you? Get out of here now!* God and the Devil were fighting for control. I took a deep breath, squeezed between the two cars in the driveway, and walked up a few stairs to reach the front door. I rang the bell, and Mrs. Johnson opened the door. She said nothing as I walked in. Not even, "Thank you for coming."

37

Dalton was standing at the top of the stairs, unshaven and unkempt. I didn't see a grown man, I saw a little boy, hurting; a boy that was lost and confused in an unfamiliar environment. Although his mother was present, the disconnection to the world he now found himself living in was obvious. With each step he took down the stairs, it was as if he was fighting to get to me, the oxygen he needed to survive. I had to remind myself I was not there to be a lifeline. I was only there to hear him out.

"I'm sorry," he said as he struggled to keep his composure.

"Why? Why did you do this?" I asked.

"I don't know. She meant nothing to me," he said.

Wow, I thought. *There it is. The words all men say after being asked why they cheat.* We should know that the issue of why men cheat has nothing to do with who *we* are. It has everything to do with who *they* are. Unfortunately, women get caught up in believing it's something we did, didn't do, said or didn't say, and generally try to blame ourselves. I should have known that Dalton's decision to step out of our relationship had nothing to do with me, but I couldn't help but feel that it did.

"It was something that happened. Do you want to call her? She'll tell you the same," he said.

"Hell no," I said.

Dalton got up, grabbed a piece of paper and a pen, and started to write. "Here," he said as he shoved the number into my hand. Although I resisted, I kind of wanted to know details, at the same time realizing more hurt lay in the specifics. I clutched my hand around the paper, not certain what I was going to do with the information.

Dalton said, "Please marry me, Anni. I want to be with you."

"I can't," I said defiantly. I stood up to leave and Dalton kept pleading with me. The doorbell rang, and Mrs. Johnson emerged from another room. She opened the door, and there stood Vaughn. As he walked in, Dalton pulled on my arm to convince me to stay. "I gotta go," I said. The more I struggled to move closer to the front door, the more stressed Dalton became. He grabbed Vaughn, begging for his help in getting me to stay. Vaughn had never seen Dalton in such a state, and he was clearly uncomfortable with the situation.

"Get off me, man!" Vaughn demanded as he pulled away from Dalton in embarrassment. "Yo, get yourself together."

Dalton moved away in shame, and even I was surprised about Vaughn's lack of sympathy. "Please don't leave," Dalton said in a more composed nature. As I stared in his eyes, a part of me wanted to stay, but the other part couldn't dishonor myself. So, I left.

Chapter 9

Dalton and I had paid for ninety percent of our wedding expenses. I was inundated with calls that questioned my decision to cancel the wedding and lose all the money we had spent. Dalton was calling me and having other people call me on his behalf. The pressure was mounting as my family's excitement increased with each day the wedding date grew closer. I was terribly confused. I loved Dalton, and I knew he loved me, but why did he do it? Why did he cheat? What did he see in her that wasn't in me? My curiosity prompted me to make the call.

"Hello," the female voice said.

"Hello," I said. "Dalton gave me your number and I wanted to talk to you."

"Yes," she said, as if she was expecting my call, already knew who I was and why I was calling. Without hesitation she told me that they were only friends and never in a relationship. She attempted to convince me that she was never interested in Dalton in a romantic way, but she did admit to one occasion that went too far. Our conversation only lasted a few minutes.

I couldn't help but wonder if the conversation had been scripted, but I thanked her for her time and hung up.

Perhaps we believe speaking to the person we feel is culpable in our partner's unfaithfulness will justify their actions. But does it really? My head was spinning as I weighed the pros and cons of my decision to call the woman and the conversation that had ensued. A day later, the girl called back.

Surprise, surprise, I thought. She couldn't handle the calm, mature manner that I had displayed during our initial exchange. I was being desired over her. Dalton wanted me. I know how the ego works. It's not humble. It's not forgiving or understanding. It doesn't thrive in authenticity. She called with the intent to hurt me and stir up the heartache I was already carrying. Although my unhappiness was not present in my words, it was flowing throughout every inch of my body.

"I want to be truthful with you," she started. "Dalton and I have actually dated a few times, and even went to the movies and dinner on several occasions. I wanted you to know everything."

"I thought you shared everything in our last conversation. Why are you telling me this now?" I quizzed.

"I didn't want to make the situation worse," she said.

"Would you say you were in a relationship with him," I asked. Silenced ensued. Was it purposeful or was this her attempt at being protective?

"We enjoyed each other's company," she said.

"Ok. Anything else you want to say?" I asked.

"We did only sleep together one time," she said.

"Ok. Yes, you've already made that clear in our last conversation. Don't call me with anything else," I said.

"I was trying to help you," she said defensively.

"I'm not the one who needs help," I said, and hung up.

She called a few more times, only to hang up. That night I jumped in my car and went to Dalton's house to confront him about the conversations I had had with this girl. He had a

Giving My Pain a Voice

surprised look on his face as his mother announced that I was there. "Can we talk privately?" I asked.

"Yes. Let me get my keys," he said. We left the house and sat in his car. "I'm happy to see you."

"Well, I can't say the same," I said. I told him about the initial phone call with this girl and our second conversation. The more I talked the more confused he appeared. Of course, he denied everything and insisted she was lying because she was mad that he wanted nothing to do with her. I told him that I didn't believe him and that my decision not to marry him remained the same. Ready to move on with canceling the wedding, I told Dalton I wanted to work out a plan with all the vendors to see how much of our money, if any, we would be able to salvage.

Dalton didn't hear anything I said as he put the key in the ignition, started the car, and began to drive off. "Let me out!" I demanded. As Dalton drove, he remained quiet. "Let me out!" I screamed.

"She's lying to you, and I have to prove it," he said determinedly.

"No! Take me back to my car!" I shouted.

"I can't lose you like this. I won't lose you like this," Dalton declared.

I was scared and felt trapped. He pulled the car into a dead end street, where the darkened woods overlooked the Parkway. When he stopped the car, he pulled out his gun, and my heart stopped as I gasped for air. Holding the gun in his lap, he said that he would not live with this pain anymore. My body trembled as I clenched my chest and struggled with the possibility that he intended to kill himself, or me, or both of us. I tried to find convincing words that could save our lives. My heart pounded, and my voice was faint. I whispered, "Dalton, put the gun down."

"Please don't leave me," he said in desperation.

My heart said *I'm not marrying you*, but my mouth said,

43

"We can work everything out. Put the gun down, and let's talk rationally."

"I'm not going to let her ruin my life," he said defiantly. "She's a liar!" he shouted, as he repeated it over and over.

"Ok. Ok. Put it down, and let's talk," I said, trying to emote calm.

Dalton finally was able to hear me, and he put the gun down. "I'm sorry," he said.

"It's ok," I said quietly as tears streamed down my face. "Let's get back to your parents' house."

As he put the car in reverse, he pleaded, "I'm really sorry. Please forgive me."

"It's ok," I said as I stared out the passenger window in disbelief. Fighting back tears, we made it safely to his parents' home. Dalton startled me as he grabbed my hand, once again saying he was sorry. I nodded my head, and we both exited the car. He kept saying he was sorry as he walked me to my car, and I kept saying it was ok. After I got in my car Dalton walked away, but I noticed he stopped to watch me drive off. As I pulled away, I was in complete shock about what had happened. I drove silently as tears streamed down my cheeks.

One block away from my home, I pulled over, clutched my face in my hands and screamed out loud in a fit of hysteria. I needed the comfort of my mother and father. I needed someone to rally behind me, like Dalton had people rallying for him in his corner. My corner was empty. There was no one to offer me a sip of water or to wipe my brow. I was alone in this fight. I was emotionally and mentally beaten and battered. I had no one to cheer me on or support me to throw in the towel. I was my own savior as I convinced myself I could overcome this. I was strong in will and might. Besides, I had no choice but to pull it together, seeing that there was no one else to do it for me.

After composing myself, I drove home. I got out of the car, entered the front door cool, calm, and collected, as if nothing had happened. I'm a pro at hiding emotions and pretending nothing is wrong even when my entire world is in shambles. I was raised to be strong in the midst of adversity. *Never let them see you sweat* was always my motto. Emotions are for the weak. Crying doesn't solve anything. Dalton's breakdown and this wedding were no different; just another problem that I would suck up and deal with. I'm smart enough to figure this out.

Chapter 10

A few weeks later, Vaughn called. Dalton and I had spent a great deal hanging out with him throughout our courtship, and Vaughn and I had developed a close brother and sister relationship. If there was anyone who had witnessed who Dalton and I were as a couple, it was Vaughn. During our conversation, Vaughn took me on a journey through my relationship with Dalton, highlighting the compatibility we shared, and pointing out how much we offered each other. He promised that our conflicts could be worked out in pre-wedding counseling, and, if necessary, post marriage therapy. I knew Vaughn had our best interest at heart, and I was open to what he had to say only because I had no one else to help me process what was happening.

I knew better than to tell Vaughn what had happened that night on the dead end street. Would it have made a difference in Vaughn's opinion of the situation and of Dalton? I never told anyone until now. People would think I was crazy, or that we both were crazy. Everyone was so desperate to get me to marry Dalton that I believed they would turn a blind eye to the safety, security and protection a woman deserves to feel with their mate. This is what I get for not involving my family. There was no one to protect me in my clouded judgement, no one to say, "Hold up. You can't marry someone that unstable. You deserve more than that."

Dalton and I had spent six years together, and I was already twenty-seven years old. Should that make any difference? Was I that desperate, to marry someone I didn't trust? How could our lives be built on dishonesty and fear? What about the embarrassment and shame of canceling the wedding, and the money we would be throwing away?

I needed someone to grant me permission not to marry Dalton. I needed an advisor to step in and say it was acceptable to let it all go. Someone should have told me that despite the money I would lose, money never trumps a life. But I had no faith in the people who were assigned to protect, guide and nurture me. I felt trapped and obligated. Too many people would be hurt and disappointed. No one could help me. Hence, my silence and my will to continue without support. *I can shoulder this. I'm strong enough to do it,* I thought.

With the pros and cons shuffling through my mind, I conceded. My gut warned me to walk away, but I couldn't. We were getting married. I allowed myself to sacrifice the promise of having a life full of happiness and truth. I willingly gave up my right to have the life I was destined for in exchange for the belief that all the details could be worked out after the wedding. With this decision, I compromised who I was. I lowered my standards to meet everyone's expectations that I would "do the right thing." Instead of standing up for myself, I ultimately silenced my voice, masked my pain, and swept it under the rug for the sake of perfection. The perfect man. The perfect wedding. The perfect life. All an illusion.

Our "I do's" were built on a foundation of hurt, pain, fear, and resentment. The polar opposite of how marriages should begin. I recall my father standing with me in the narthex of the church prior to the ceremony. He asked, "You sure you want to do this? If not, we can walk out of here right now." Everything in me wanted to say, "Yes! Get me out of here!" Instead, I walked down that aisle, prepared to lie to myself, Dalton, and our families and friends. We both stood before God, going through the motions, and even had the audacity of lighting unity candles. We participated in the honored tradition of jumping the broom, which signified we were ready to be man and wife. All the people who promised to stand by us and hold us together were witnesses to the lies we told that day. Everyone on Dalton's side of the church knew about the dysfunction that occurred prior to the wedding, but they smiled on cue. On my side, they basked in the glory of seeing their baby girl, sister, niece, and friend accomplish yet another goal in life. Little did they know our marriage and our future was on a path straight to hell.

Anyone who has built a sand castle on the beach can attest, anything built on sand will crumble. We entered our first year of marriage oblivious to the devastation and destruction we would cause each other. My submission gave Dalton a false sense of hope, believing that all had been forgiven. Paradoxically, I was filled with an unspeakable amount of unforgiveness, which I carried on my sleeve like a badge of honor. My devastation was prevalent in my walk, my talk, and my approach to our marriage. I didn't respect him. I didn't trust him. I was afraid of him. I was quietly suffocating. The vibrant spirit I once had was no longer present. My soul had been murdered by the reckless decisions I had made.

As I watched each year of my marriage pass by, I slowly lost oxygen and the drive to resuscitate my life. From the moment I said, "I do", I failed. A world of darkness took over, which wasn't fair to me or the two beautiful children I brought into this world. I lay down and allowed myself to be used as a doormat by Dalton's friends and family, as my compromise was seen by them as weakness. It was as if permission to treat me like dirt was granted. My strength and the respect I had worked so hard to build up were torn down.

Dalton, suffering from his own demons, was no match for the evil that took over our marriage, our home, and each of us individually. We attempted to resolve our issues in therapy to no avail. We couldn't find a therapist that wasn't fascinated and sidetracked by Dalton's adoption story. They were always more intrigued with the details of Dalton's personal history instead of analyzing how his adoption and feelings of abandonment played so negatively throughout his life and into our marriage.

Dalton was broken way before he met me. His brokenness was the catalyst for my life ending up shattered as well. Instead of exploring how our upbringing played a significant role in determining who we became as adults, the therapists wanted to know how we found his birth family and what that union was like. I knew Dalton's pain; it was deep and it destroyed him inside and out. I understood his pain but I had no clue how to help him. I had my own problems as I struggled with all he had done to me, and questioned why I allowed myself to be in this situation in the first place.

We had become masters at hiding our suffering. Despite our efforts to seek professional counseling, we were not equipped with the tools needed to get us through our despair. We would smile and portray ourselves as the perfect happy couple, but behind closed doors, everything fell apart. My attempt to pull myself together every day was like trying to pull a one hundred pound boulder from the bottom of the ocean. I was emotionally dead, from my head to the soles of my feet. My lifeless body seemed to float around from place to place in an effort to manage as a mother, wife and professional. My soul died and was buried the day I got married. I was no longer the pillar of strength that people knew me to have been. My friendships were dissolving, and my ambition had disappeared. I spent most days grasping at straws, trying to function.

"What happened to you?" Emily would often ask. "Ever since you had Alisa, something has changed."

I didn't have the nerve to tell Emily or anyone else the truth. No one except Kameron and Marie knew what had happened during our engagement. I was embarrassed being *that* woman, who turns a blind eye to a man's faults, and doesn't leave or seek what she needs. You know the woman I'm talking about - the one who knows their man cheated on them but decides to stay with him anyway. The woman who is abused and makes excuses. The woman who says, "But he loves me and I love him," and yet she fears him. How could I possibly explain ME, the independent pillar of strength, falling victim to all that? I'm not the kind of person who would deal with such foolishness, so why did I accept it with Dalton? What made him so deserving that I had to give up who I was for him?

Chapter 11

Our married life was full of complicated challenges. Aside from the negative influences around us, we made repeated attempts to deal with our unresolved issues. As with any relationship, we struggled through the ups and downs, but the downs were exacerbated by the weight we carried. Dalton remained haunted by his past and his inability to shield me from being the recipient of his suffering. He was never physically abusive, but our doors and walls would beg to differ.

As our marriage deteriorated, Dalton's fear of not being with our kids and me was too much for him to bear. Being adopted, a blood-lined family meant everything. An argument for Dalton wasn't simply an argument, and he viewed every quarrel as an attempt to dissolve his family. The thought of being without us was not an option. This realization heightened my fear, as Dalton was not ever going to live, or allow anyone else to live, if we couldn't be together. I was afraid to leave him, although everything in me wanted to. My kids and I were not living the life I had always envisioned for us. I know there is no perfect marriage or ideal family, but we were so far removed from any resemblance of happiness that I was unable to see our way out of this with a good ending.

Already haunted by my own self-inflicted demons, my life became much more complicated in 2002 when my brother was involved in a terrible motorcycle wreck that changed the dynamics of my family. His accident rocked me to the core. Owen, my brother, and I were close. Even though he was three and a half years older than me, I was his defender. I was his advocate. I was his secret keeper. He was the typical older brother who tried to shield me from harm.

When Owen's accident happened and the severity of his condition was revealed, I was in shock. I needed someone to revive me with those paddles doctors use to send electric shock into a person when their heart stops. Clear…one, two, three. Clear…one, two, three. To no avail. My imaginary defibrillation could not save me from the nightmare when I was told my brother was paralyzed and would remain dependent on long-term care for the duration of his life.

Owen's wife and my family became strained within a few days after the accident. Like any accident, there are blurred lines as to what one may think is best. It's possible that a person may understand their spouse much better and more intimately than the parents and might have a clearer idea about what is needed to make one more comfortable. But when the surviving spouse checks out emotionally, mentally, and physically, what then? My brother's motionless body lay in the balance between the love of his wife and the love of his family.

I was no longer my brother's keeper. I was unable to advocate for him as I always had over the years. I was unable to protect him and advise him in decisions that were in his best interest. My parents and I had been purposely shut out of my brother's life with a stroke of a pen. Outside of visiting him for the seven years he lay dormant in a nursing home, our voices were silenced and we were prevented from contributing to decisions that would prolong his life or not, enhance it or not, or be a part of any decisions in relation to the quality of his life.

Owen had to have a tracheotomy and had a breathing tube in his windpipe. Unable to speak without the aid of a speaking valve inserted by a respiratory therapist, my brother was silent. He'd become frustrated with his failed attempts to mouth words, hoping we would understand. But when we didn't, boy, did he get angry. The speaking valve would have made verbally engaging with him so much easier, but considering the device caused mucus to build up in the trach and required suctioning, he most often refused to utilize it. The procedure to clear the trach caused him to choke and appeared to be very painful. He would only put the valve in to speak to his son or my children during our visits.

My brother lived a miserable life for seven years prior to his death. During our visits, he watched my children grow from the corner of his eyes. He suffered, and we suffered. Owen had been a vibrant spirit who lived life by the seat of his pants, and he was confined to a bed without the ability to move any part of his body, with the exception of shaking his head side to side or up and down. This type of existence extinguishes the light in one's soul.

My voice was no longer effective, as it had always been when we were kids. Owen's own flesh and blood couldn't advocate for him, as our hands were tied by HIPPA laws, control and egos. The conflict with my sister-in-law and her family divided us, as often occurs when an unexpected life-changing event happens. Instead of working together to do what was best for Owen, his wife took control while his flesh and blood family observed as bystanders. Resentment and feelings of helplessness consumed our lives as we watched my brother slowly and painfully deteriorate. My brother's death further solidified my already existing mortality. He took a piece of me with him when he departed this world that has yet to return. Dalton tried to support me through my loss, but he was the source of it too. How could he help me heal from so much destruction when he contributed to my misery? I resented him even trying. So much had been taken from me, and I found myself in a world that was not a pleasant place.

My brother's death pushed me further into a depression as I struggled to maintain the sanity I barely had a grip on anyway. I couldn't hold myself up even if I tried, but I was still responsible for being a mother through it all. Unfortunately, I couldn't give my kids everything they needed to thrive in a healthy environment. Our marriage was an exact replica of our parents' marriage, and all the ingredients needed to nurture and grow a healthy and happy family were absent long before our own existence into the world. Generational patterns were present as we raised our kids. It wasn't fair that my children were forced to live in an isolated world because their parents were plagued with so much dysfunction and the inability to pull ourselves out of the pit that was becoming increasingly deep. Who was going to save us from ourselves? No one even knew we needed saving. No one knew what existed behind our doors. As a family, we were so broken. Shattered to its core.

When my brother lay in a hospital bed for seven years, people would always tell me to pray and ask God for help in healing him. Ask God for help? Why would I do that? I had been living in hell since I got married, and if there were a God wouldn't He have stepped in by now? I thought it was exactly like those Bible thumpers to believe that God was the answer to everything. If that was the case, why wasn't my brother healed? Why would he suffer like he did? Why would my mother lose both of her sisters (one being her identical twin) to cancer? Why would her brother die while saying his prayers to a God that is supposed to heal? Why am I trapped in quicksand up to my neck? Where's God's help?

There was no way God was present in the misery that was happening. I was angry with God and blamed Him for letting my brother live in a terrible state; for allowing his wife to dishonor the vows she took "in sickness and in health"; for my mother's suffering, as she helplessly watched her son's life slowly slip away from our grasp; for leaving me as an only child; for stealing my joy and burdening me with intolerable pain; for robbing my kids of the excitement that only Uncle Owen could offer; for allowing the division between Owen's wife and my family, which resulted in me not seeing my nephew since two years before Owen died. I was denied getting to see him grow up. Why would God allow such things? How could He let this suffering go on? I blamed God for destroying my family. For rendering my mother emotionally crippled as a result of the emotional pain and loss she experienced. What kind of God does that?

I did not grow up in a church. I only went as an adult because Dalton was going sporadically. My father taught me that I didn't have to go to church to believe in God. So I didn't. I believed He existed, but I didn't believe He had ever done anything special for me. God let my brother suffer and die, and He took all the people who ever loved my mother. I was mad at him! The roots of resentment, hurt, anger and frustration grew deeper into the soil of my body and my mind. This time, the roots were anchoring themselves in preparation for a lifetime of growth, unless something was done to change the course of my life.

I walked through life in a daze, numb to the world around me. I missed my brother, and I felt the loneliness of now being an only child. My mother was filled with agony that she would never acknowledge, despite my efforts to elicit her to help me deal with my feelings. We could have shared our sorrow over Owen, but she was the master of masking her emotions to convince herself that she was all right.

The heaviness of trying to cope was weighing me down. Dalton and I both carried a sense of darkness around us like a cloak. Although we surprisingly were able to continue successfully in our careers, our home life was a wreck. We were not mature enough to put our thoughts and feelings into words and work through them, but instead we acted out our frustrations and hurt towards one another. We tried to shield our kids from the turmoil, but everyone knows that children hear and see everything despite attempts to protect them.

Short-tempered, hostile, demeaning, disrespectful insults were hurled around as easily as "I love you" would be spoken in a normally functioning household. I hated my life and everything in it. This wasn't supposed to be my life. I was definitely on the wrong path, but how was I to get off this road and onto the right one? I tried to push through by acting "normal", by joining the PTA and immersing myself in work. Anything I could do to distract myself from what was really go on was better than sitting idle in misery. Dalton and I were living two separate lives. We had mastered the art of being around each other with no real investment in our marital growth. I was no longer interested in being married and continuing the charade, and it was time to work on an exit strategy to prepare myself and my kids for getting out alive.

Chapter 12

After sixteen and a half years, I had no idea what my life was going to look like after my marriage ended. I hadn't shared the details of my dysfunctional life with anyone except my friends, Emily and Kameron. No one knew the real story. My parents were clueless to the turmoil I had been enduring. Where would I live? Would I stay in our home and ask Dalton to leave? What job could I find? Where would I send my kids to school? The thoughts were overwhelming me, and I started to carry the additional stress of unanswered questions.

A co-worker asked me one day what was going on, noting that I seemed withdrawn and distracted. "I have a lot on my plate," was my response.

"Take it to God," she said confidently.

The puzzled look on my face was priceless. I wanted to say, Do you know what I've been through? Where was God then? "God?" I asked.

"Yes, God. You do believe in God, right?" she asked.

"Well, yeah. But He hasn't done anything for me," I said in a matter of fact tone. She was flabbergasted at my response.

You can always tell the people who were raised going to church, because there is never any question when you talk about the likes of God. I explained that I had not grown up attending church, with the exception of a few times in the summer when I visited my Aunt Ruth in North Carolina. When I was there, I went to her church, or my grandmother's church, Bethel AME, for Sunday school.

"Oh," she said with a surprised look. She began telling me about God, sharing various Bible stories, and noted the prominent apostles throughout the Bible. She emphasized the people of strength like Job, Peter, Paul, and most importantly, Jesus. The stories she told me over the course of the next few months were influential in getting me interested in going to church. She brought me a Bible, although I did have one from when I was eight years old, but it was a children's Bible. I returned to Dalton's childhood church, the same church we had been married in, and I started going to church every Sunday, alone.

I began to work on myself. I started applying the scriptures and principles I was learning in church and Bible study to my life. I was finding some peace within, yet my emotional separation from Dalton was growing, along with my past struggles that continued to exist. We disagreed on everything, from how we operated our household to the responsibilities of the children. I was determined to get myself out of the dysfunctional cycle that had become a routine in my life. I owed it to myself and to my kids, to right my wrongs, and turn this horrible adversity into a path toward success. I wasn't exactly sure how to do that, but my determination to break free was becoming stronger.

In addition to getting more involved in the church, I started watching the OWN network and found *Oprah's Lifeclass* and *Master Class* series quite intriguing. Each person featured in programs talked about overcoming adversity, and the perseverance it took to get them to the success they achieved. However, it wasn't until I watched *Oprah's Master Class* two-part series on Oprah's own life that it struck a chord with me. Oprah talked candidly about her life, upbringing, and the obstacles she faced along her road to success. She faced unthinkable odds and endured great hardship and emotional pain, but through it all, she became one of the most successful media moguls to date. She uses her life experiences as lessons for others, to teach them what she has learned. Isn't that what the Bible talks about? *Serve one another humbly in love. For the entire law is fulfilled in keeping this one command: "Love your neighbor as yourself."* (Galatians 5:13-14 NIV.)

I didn't have the courage to leave my job, because I had been working on an exit plan from my marriage, and there was no way I could afford to be unemployed. So, I ignored the call for some time, only to be tormented because of my ignorance to be obedient when God calls you to do something and you refuse.

The more I tried to move closer to God, the more I felt convicted about my choices. I was trying to break free from the dark cloud that had been hovering since our marriage. I had become lost and confused, and work had become a huge burden, despite the fulfillment I received from it. It was time to leave, but I couldn't understand why or how I was going to take care of my kids and myself if I left. *It's time to tap into your purpose for being here*, the voice would say. *You have to leave your job first*. What was this voice anyway? Was it my own thoughts? Was it God speaking to me?

I often felt tense and uneasy. My parents would call me and say I sounded out of sorts. It was strange that they sensed a difference now, but they had been unable to detect what was going on over the past few years. I found myself going stir crazy as my parents would try to convince me that leaving my job was a foolish idea. They said, "You're making good money and it's close to home. You can't leave your job until you find another one."

"Why can't you hear me?" I said in desperation. "I *have* to leave my job. I *want* to leave my job. I *need* to leave my job." I had been the director of an outpatient medical program for senior citizens and young disabled adults. I was happy there and had been able to climb the ladder of success, but it was time to leave. I wanted more for my life, my kids, and myself. God was telling me there was more to life. He was preparing a bigger platform for me.

Was it completely irrational to leave my job? I had saved up quite a bit of money to sustain me for the next couple of years. I could continue to handle my financial responsibilities at home without putting any financial burden on Dalton. Dalton was not in favor of me leaving my job, but he was never in favor of anything that jeopardized the false foundation he believed we had. I was ready to let it all go and, for the first time in my life, throw caution to the wind. I watched *Oprah's Master Class* again one night and typed up my letter of resignation. I was being awakened to the life I was supposed to have. I was finally opening my eyes and coming to life again.

I had a gut feeling that my purpose in life was so much bigger than what I was doing. I no longer felt comfortable in my job, and I realized God was trying to prepare me for the next step. I was destined for greatness, but the greatness He wanted for me could not be achieved at my current job. He needed to free me and be open to new possibilities. Despite my conviction that I needed to leave my job, fear was taking over and I doubted my decision.

I placed the letter of resignation on my desk and looked at it for weeks. Was I doing the right thing? I'd never been without a job or unable to financially care for my family. Was I being selfish? I blamed my tendency to overthink and analyze everything as one of the terrible traits that consume Virgos. Perfectionists incarnate. Virgos want every decision to be perfect, with perfect outcomes. My Virgo-ism was obsessive and overshadowing any possible thought of positivity. So, when I felt my back was up against the wall, I called my friend, Emily.

"Pull the trigger on that job, and let the chips fall where they may!" she said. "You're the only person I know who could hoard money. I'm sure you have planned this all out. Just do it! Go for it!"

Go for it! Those were the words I needed to hear, someone to say, "Yes! You can make it. You can do it." Why did I think I needed permission to do the things I believed were right for me? Where was my self-confidence? Why did I depend on Emily to confirm my choices? Why couldn't Dalton or my parents see I needed their support? *Who cares,* I thought. Regardless of what tipped the scales on that day, in that moment, I had the resolve that I needed.

I grabbed the resignation letter, which had been sealed in a white envelope on my desk, and headed down the long hallway. Without hesitation, I placed the envelope in the administrator's mailbox and walked away. The freedom I felt was so liberating! I was desperate to claim my life back, and I knew this would be the catalyst. With the submission of my resignation, I was demanding the return of my independence, and freedom from the bondage that had entangled my life. I was escaping the darkness of the meager existence I had been enduring as a result of Dalton's demons. I was breaking free and rescuing my kids in the process. Wherever the path might lead, I was going there. *I'm on my way!* So I thought.

Chapter 13

I was excited to be starting another chapter in my life. This was going to be the very first time where there were no goals and no plans. I had always been a planner. Every move was calculated and analyzed for the best desirable outcome. Remember, I'm a Virgo.

Everyone thought I had gone crazy for leaving my job. We're brought up believing that going to college and securing a good job with benefits and a pension is the end-all-be-all. Nobody in their right mind was leaving a secure job for a fantasy world. A world where you take a step and have no idea what happens next. No one in my family could wrap their heads around this concept and they thought I was having a mental breakdown. Being proactive and independent, I secured enough of my own finances to carry my household responsibilities without flaw. This newfound freedom felt so good.

I was able to pick my daughter up from school, make her snacks, and prepare dinner with ease. The life of a full time working mother became a distant memory, and I relished the discovery of the benefits I gained. I had time to slow things down and cement a new foundation to our lives. We had become a family on a mouse wheel. Spinning in circles, rushing from here to there, and trying to juggle so many things at once caused us to lose sight of what was important.

Growing up, neither Dalton nor I ever had meals as a family at the dinner table. This is a family staple that has been missing among families for many years. Gathering to share in each other's company, impart wisdom about life, or discussing current situations plaguing our children had become an important part of our everyday life. In my effort to bring our family together, it was important to create an environment that forced us to engage in a traditional manner as opposed to text messaging or other digital means. Now was the perfect opportunity to show my kids how a family operates. Dinner was already prepared when Dalton and the kids arrived home from work and school. Alisa, our daughter who is four years older than her brother Carter, helped me bring the last items to the table, and as we ate our meal, we would talk about our day. The dinner table was a place to gather and express ourselves honestly, and to be mindful of others sharing their thoughts. My efforts were having a positive effect on the kids. I needed them to be able to use their words to convey their feelings because I knew leaving Dalton was not going to be easy on any of us. Our family was reaping some benefits as we attempted to communicate more effectively.

Although I had begun to make many strides at creating a good solid foundation for our kids, my marriage remained in disarray. As a distraction to deal with the stress of our marriage, I would often join my college friend, Terri, and her girlfriends who loved to travel and experience new adventures. We'd make plans several times throughout the year and in 2012 we decided to vacation at Miraval Resort and Spa in Tucson, Arizona. Terri usually came up with the vacation idea and planned everything. She normally invited me and her best friend, Michelle, and occasionally other friends from college or work. I had never been to the western United States, as all of my vacations thus far were to the Caribbean.

Trips with Terri were always fun, and they provided a temporary escape from home. I would take any chance I could to get away from the heaviness that was prevalent in my life. Miraval couldn't have come at a more perfect time. I had left my job and awakened to the exciting possibilities that were waiting for me. I told Dalton about the trip after Terri, Michelle and I booked our flights and made the reservations. I really wasn't concerned about how he felt. The kids always spent the summers with my parents, so I didn't have to worry about them.

Miraval was described as a wellness spa, and I was excited, to say the least. I had been watching the OWN network's encouraging programs, and I was ready to tap into my awakened spirit. I was on a new life journey and was open to whatever was to come my way. I perused the Miraval website and jotted down all the activities I wanted to experience.

The women going with me to Miraval had made it known during the reservation that they wanted to have their own individual rooms. I questioned why, being that in the past we had always shared a room without any problems. Their explanation was that for the expense of a luxury spa, they felt it more appropriate to have their own rooms. They were accustomed to traveling alone and staying in hotels by themselves, but I wasn't. I had never traveled anywhere alone! This would be a new challenge for me and, although I was very much hesitant, I agreed. I needed to get used to being without Dalton. What better way to start than with this trip? My fears were pushed to the brink, but I had to be ready for life as a single woman.

The morning of the trip, I felt extremely anxious, almost fearful. Anxiety was a new feeling for me, but I thought it could be part of my excitement. Maybe it was the dread of being in a room by myself. Dalton and I stopped by to pick up Terri and Michelle from Terri's house, and he assisted them with putting their luggage in the truck. As Dalton drove us to the airport, an unexpected feeling of sadness washed over me. I wasn't sure why, but it felt like I was leaving something behind. Something was pulling at my emotions, and I felt afraid.

As we pulled up to the Delta terminal at LaGuardia Airport, I tried to search my heart for what I was feeling. With little time to spare, I hopped out the truck with everyone else and tucked away my feeling of apprehension. After Dalton removed our luggage from the truck, we were ready to get on our way. As Michelle and Terri stood on the curb near their suitcases, Dalton embraced me. I held onto him a little longer than usual as the two women looked on.

Dalton asked, "Everything good?"

I said, "Yup," and off we went.

Everything didn't feel good. Was I making the right decision to leave Dalton? How would he handle life without me? I was sad and confused. I had juggled the dysfunction for so long that I was unaware of what life would feel like outside of that fear, pain, hurt and resentment that had ruled our lives.

Chapter 14

When we arrived at Miraval, we immediately noticed the entire resort was tranquil and very Zen-like. We checked in, and we were escorted to our rooms. Michelle had a king size bed, and Terri and I each had standard rooms with two queen sized beds. The rooms were spacious, rustic in design, with calming earth colors and comfortable amenities.

After we unpacked and were settled in, it was too early for dinner so we explored the grounds to peek at some of the amenities we'd read about. As we walked around the peaceful atmosphere, we stumbled upon a Zen garden with a labyrinth. My friend, Leann, had originally introduced me to the mystique of labyrinths. Leann practiced a holistic approach to healing and was instrumental in helping me think outside the box. I loved her for opening my eyes to another perspective and always supporting my well-being. I came to realize that the power to move forward lives within me, and resources such as labyrinths and essential oils are only vehicles to propel me toward the path God had for me.

The labyrinth at Miraval was a circular rock formation,

creating a walking mediation path. As with my first experience with a labyrinth, we walked in silence, following each other in single file. As I proceeded on the path, I instantly found myself praying. I felt a peace overwhelm me, and my spirit felt open. As the three of us walked silently in a rhythmic pattern, the fine sand and pebbles crunched under our feet with every step. In that moment, I realized why I needed to be at Miraval. This place was going to be a place of transformation, a re-birth, an awakening of my soul and spirit. I was ready!

Mindfulness. Living in the moment. Purpose. Awakening. Inner peace. I started to become open to a completely new world. No one in my family had ever talked about this world, probably because they had never discovered it either. Here was a space where people openly shared their emotions and tapped into a much deeper part of the self which often goes unnoticed. Examining who you are and why you are here on earth. Exploring hurt, pain, and the reasons why you do what you do.

As I began to absorb this new environment, I relaxed and had such a sense of freedom. God was touching my heart. Coming to Miraval, I was physically removed from the source of my pain, but I was still emotionally connected. *Inhale slowly and exhale freely*, my mind said.

We walked back to our rooms to change for dinner, and when I opened my door I was greeted by a gecko that scurried across the floor. WHY, LORD? WHY? I have a serious phobia of reptiles, and for one to be in my room on my very first time staying in a room alone was the ultimate slap in the face. I ran out and banged on Terri's door, which was directly next to mine. She opened the door and asked, "What's wrong?"

I cried, "There is no way I'm staying in that room. There is a lizard in there!"

She laughed and asked, "Where?" She came back to my door and we both watched as it ran across the floor again and into the bathroom area (of all places). She looked in the bathroom, but she couldn't find it. "Call the front desk," she said.

"You call the front desk!" I exclaimed. "I'm not going near that phone."

Terri made the call and waited with me until a maintenance worker arrived. He said geckos are a common sight around the resort, and they can't hurt me. *Yeah right.* He checked the bathroom, and it was gone. He said he believed it had gone down the drain in the shower, but he tried to assure me that I would be fine. REALLY!? *I'm far from fine. I'm in this room alone and with a gecko of all things. I'm not fine!*

Terri shrugged it off and said, "Girl, you'll be fine. Get dressed because we're going to dinner soon." I begged her to allow me to stay in her room since she had two queen beds also, and she refused. "Get dressed!" She left my room and I was alone. I stood by the entrance to my room for at least fifteen minutes, not sure which way to move. I was scared out of my mind. All the peace I had experienced thirty minutes earlier was out the window. I was paralyzed with fear and seriously questioning how I was going to survive the next five days, and four dark nights. *Oh, my God, do they come out in groups at night?* I couldn't breathe.

I tiptoed over to my luggage, picked it up, and placed it on the bench close to the bed. I was afraid the gecko might have crawled into my suitcase, and I was yanking my clothes out the bag while jumping around to avoid contact in case one appeared. I found myself praying and asking God to help me through this fear. I had a lot of nerve praying to someone I had cut out of my life for years, and I wasn't confident He heard me or intended to help. I finally got the strength to enter the bathroom, and I grabbed a hand towel to place over the shower drain. I nearly cried the whole time I was in the shower and rushed to get out of the bathroom. The gecko didn't make another appearance while I was getting dressed. Thank God!

We all met in Michelle's room and they teased me about

my new roommate. Although I laughed along, I was petrified. As we walked over to the dining area, we noticed a huge, dark cloud descending upon the resort. We heard other guest saying the storms here during monsoon season could be violent, and they advised us to take cover soon.

It was not yet time for our dinner reservation, so we decided to walk around. We discovered a class in progress, and a sculptor who had created beautiful works of art invited us to join in. Each piece of his art represented a journey, and he wanted to share his experiences with us.

The menacing clouds we had seen in the distance materialized into a fierce thunderstorm with severe lightning. I've never been a fan of storms, and as a child, I would cower behind my parents for safety. My fears were seriously being tested on this first day. The power was knocked out, and we sat through the class in the dark. The sculptor took the opportunity to get to know us a little and welcomed us to Miraval, providing some calm to the scary situation.

After the storm, we proceeded to the resort restaurant, and luckily, the electricity came back on. Dinner was light, yet filling, and we were excited about the days to come. After our meal, we signed up for some individual activities for the next day. I signed up for the Desert Tightrope Challenge, but Terri and Michelle made other choices. Apparently, I had a different concept of a girls' get-away than them because they were more interested in doing things alone than together. Prior to retiring for the night, we enjoyed a light snack and drinks. Everything shut down fairly early, and the resort was like a ghost town by 7:00 pm. As the locals did, we retired for the night, and in the quiet of my room, I took time to review all the amenities of the resort.

Chapter 15

I was in a gorgeous luxury resort, with dozens of amazing opportunities, two companions, and every possibility for an unforgettable vacation. To tell the truth, I was scared out of my mind. As I grappled with my fear of being in a room alone, I couldn't help but wonder, *Is this what life will be like without Dalton's presence?* Was this God's sense of humor - to give me an idea of what single life was going to entail?

I didn't sleep much as I tossed and turned all night long, worrying about my future, not to mention the fear that the gecko might make another appearance. I awoke around 4:00 am, which was unusually early for me, but then I remembered the three hour time difference between home and Arizona. After showering and getting prepared for my morning activity, I found myself in mediation as I sat on the edge of the bed. *Stop making excuses,* an inner voice was telling me. *Believe you are worthy of great things. Get moving on the path of greatness!*

Why was I thinking these thoughts? Ignoring the randomness of my mind, I gathered my Miraval tote bag and left my room. The resort was buzzing with people by 6:00 am. The breakfast included steel-cut oats, fresh fruit, and everything healthy. The three of us met in the dining room, and over our breakfast, I told Terri that I had changed my mind about doing the Desert Tightrope Challenge. She encouraged me to go and said, "You'll be fine."

Why was I feeling like a child? What was happening that made me afraid to do anything alone? Was the fact that I was contemplating leaving Dalton playing to my psyche? My friends were so independent, and I had thought I was too, until this trip.

I was anxious again as I reluctantly went to the meeting area and gathered with the other participants of the challenge. I filled up my Miraval water bottle and followed along with the group of eight others who had signed up. Apparently, most of the people in the group knew each other, so I trailed behind them. It gave me a chance to realize how proud I was of myself for making it through the night in the room alone. My focus was not to stress about anything anymore: being alone, the gecko, or Dalton. I wanted to use this opportunity at Miraval to cleanse myself of the fears that held me back. Many of my fears seemed to be confronting me during this trip, but I couldn't let them get the best of me. God was trying to get my attention. Complaining and allowing my fears to take hold were going to drown out His voice. *Get it together!*

Controlling fear and not letting fear control me was what the Desert Tightrope Challenge meant for me. Some of my fears I had been secretly carrying for a long time. I'm strong. I'm independent. I'm Superwoman. But yet, I was afraid. I found myself asking God to help me trust Him and to increase my faith in Him because I believed He had failed me. I wanted to put the past behind me and move confidently into my future.

The support of the eight strangers who participated with me on the challenge was great. The instructor, Joshua, let us decide the order of who would go first. I briefly thought, *In a million years, I would never volunteer to go first.* I didn't analyze or calculate as I normally would, and I quickly blurted out that I would take the lead. Once the order was established, I met Joshua at the ladder. He facilitated as a therapist would in helping me figure out my thoughts. "What do you hope to accomplish on this challenge?" he asked.

"I don't know," I said anxiously.

"Some people want to overcome their fear of heights. Some use the tightrope as a metaphor. Others push themselves to complete a task," he said. "What are you looking for?"

This question took me by surprise considering I viewed the challenge as a physical activity and hadn't considered anything beyond that. "I'm not sure yet," I admitted.

Joshua patiently said, "Ok. Let's get you started. Maybe something will come to you while you're up there." He checked my harness for safety and assisted with my hard hat. I asked if I was attached to the belay, the secured rope he controlled, and he reassured me that I was good to go.

I placed my foot on the first peg of a tall wooden pole, similar to a light pole. Step by step, I quickly climbed the pegged pole without hesitation. I'm not normally afraid of heights, but I was thirty-five feet in the air! Up close, I could see the tightrope was extremely thin. The fear of failing to make it across was overwhelming, but I was determined. I said a prayer to the new God who I was becoming close friends with and asked Him to protect me and keep me safe.

As I stepped out on the tightrope and attempted to reach the first rope to grip, I felt afraid. I'm normally very adventurous, but this experience was like no other. Numerous ropes and lines make up the tightrope. The parts of the rig began to move and sway with my weight, and I realized this uncertainty was symbolic of life. Although life can be challenging, scary, unpredictable and unsteady, God keeps you focused, as long as you're totally focused on Him. With the eight strangers enthusiastically cheering me on, and my focus on God, I took one step at a time.

With each hanging rope spread various distances apart, I

was slow and steady. There was a brief moment when I lost sight of God because I was more focused on grabbing the rope. I began to wobble, lose my footing, and almost fell backward. I yelled, "I'm going down!" My companions encouraged me, and I prayed to God for balance, and He granted it. With His help, I completed my task. I made it all the way to the end of the challenge, thankful for the support of my cheering partners. I was happy to be there to give each of them encouragement as they faced the challenge after me.

The Desert Tightrope Challenge showed me how to increase my faith and trust in the Lord. As long as I remained focused on Him - trusting and believing He would never fail me - I would be fine. The moment I didn't focus, I lost my balance and almost fell off the rope. I had been asking God to increase my faith and strengthen my trust since my brother died. As I meditated on my tightrope experience, I realized that I was able to overcome my fears. If staying focused on the Lord could get me to the other side of the tightrope without falling off, He could provide what I needed for the rest of my life.

I was so proud of myself. I was more proud of completing the Desert Tightrope Challenge than any other accomplishment in my life, which might seem weird. You see, this challenge had everything to do with living outside the box. With God's support and the backing of loved ones, I was able to conquer the great fears in my life that were holding me hostage. This challenge helped me prove that I could stay in a room at a resort alone and not be afraid. I could be comfortable with me. With faith and trust in the Lord, I could accomplish anything.

Years ago, God had placed a vision of greatness in my heart. With the tightrope experience and the clarity it provided, I believe I am able to achieve it! I am a woman of service and I can't wait to live out my purpose in this life. I no longer want to live a routine state of mind. I desire to be open to all the possibilities God has destined for me. Thank you, God, for being patient with me and not throwing me away when I denounced you. Thank you for giving me the courage to leave my job and creating this trip to reconnect with me. Thank you, God, for opening my heart for an awesome adventure, and the lessons you helped me learn.

Chapter 16

On my walk back to my room after the challenge, I saw Terri sitting on a bench outside of her room, and I thanked her for pushing me to do the Desert Tightrope Challenge. She was preparing to go to her activity, so I went to lunch alone, basking in the experience that had taken place. I saw some of the people who were in my group, and they told me they were so proud of me. *Wow*, I thought. I had never had anyone tell me they were proud of me, and I felt the genuineness of their praise. Yes, of course, my parents told me when I had accomplishments over the years, but I don't recall them ever actually watching my struggles. To bear witness of me fighting to stay on that tightrope and reach beyond normal limits to make it from one hanging rope to another was an experience my parents were never privy to. I kept my struggles to myself. My parents never knew if anything was troubling me since I would never share that part of myself with anyone. Remember, I was Superwoman, and she never struggles.

I was growing comfortable being on my own, since most people visiting the resort cherished the solitude. It was a time to rejuvenate. I joined a group in yoga mediation, and it was extremely relaxing. I had to learn to breathe without feeling like I was hyperventilating and not let my mind wander. These methods were new to me, and I vowed to practice at least twice a day. Michelle and Terri met me for dinner and we shared stories about the day's adventures. We were so exhausted from getting up early and the day's activities that we were ready to retire for the evening.

The days flew by, and we enjoyed other activities and the beautiful scenery around the resort. Michelle and I went to a psychic group reading and participated in a team oriented pool challenge. The three of us spent time in the sauna, did meditations and enjoyed yoga. We participated together in the Equine Experience, which was a unique form of therapy that utilizes horses who could detect the energy one puts out towards others. If our energy was calm, the horse would respond to us in kind. If our energy was too forceful or if our intentions were not sound, the horse reacted negatively. It was a good way of learning to stay in the moment and to make sure our intentions were pure and purposeful. On our last full day, I woke up feeling excited as the three of us were going to participate in the Swing and a Prayer Challenge. As with most experiences at Miraval, the activity was scheduled for 6:30 am to avoid the hot sun. We walked to the challenge course and chatted about this activity being featured on Oprah's show.

The challenges at Miraval were designed to push us beyond our comfort zone and open our mind and heart space to a different perspective. The facilitator, Mark, explained the purpose of the course, which truly lived up to its name - A Swing and a Prayer. This was definitely a group-oriented effort. Some of the group had to support the ladder, and there was a rope connected to the participant that was pulled by every member in the group in order to lift the person to the desired height.

As we were hoisted thirty-five feet in the air by the efforts of our group members, we said aloud what we wanted to let go of. We prayed and let go of the rope that held us in place, which caused us to free fall into a full-fledged swinging motion. Without the effort and support of the group, we went nowhere. This was a team building exercise and our success was dependent on our team's support. There was communication between everyone to ensure safety, and Mark was there to help each person work through any obstacles. Some people had a fear of heights, while others were afraid of letting go. The facilitator assisted people, not only physically, but also helping them realize the obstacles in their life that needed to be let go. Everyone's experience was different, as well as their challenges or obstacles. I positioned myself somewhere in the middle of the participants, as others wanted to go ahead of me.

I watched each member of our group take their turn, and I was flooded with thoughts about what I needed to let go. My brother's death. My failed marriage and the stress I had carried for years. My independence and the lack of support I received from family and friends. My Aunt Ruth's death, which took an enormous toll on me because she was like my second mother. My Aunt Alice, who I always felt protected me, losing her battle with lung cancer. My Uncle Jack, dying while saying his prayers one morning. My cousin Louie, who sustained my mother during my brother's confinement in the long-term facility, only to find him dead two hours before my brother took his last breath. My Uncle Bernie, who loved my family and my kids as if they were his own grandkids.

All these responsibilities and burdens had weighed heavily on me. I had been carrying all of this like a stone around my neck. The shouldered obligation to keep everything together no matter what. Never let them see you sweat! Keep your walls up. Never show your vulnerable side. Otherwise, people will destroy you. Be perfect at all cost. I have been hard and strong my whole life. Quiet but aggressive when needed and I could verbally cut you down into sawdust. Why am I carrying this weight? I'm holding it down for everyone else, but who's holding it down for me? I'm being a parent to my parents, a mother to my husband, and a mother to my own children. But who takes care of me?

As my thoughts continued to run rampant, it was my turn to approach the ladder. I moved to the base, placed my right foot on the first step, and then the left on the second step. I repeated the motions until I was at the top of the ladder. Mark, our wonderful facilitator, locked me into position and then lowered himself down to the ground. The team shouted, "Anni, are you ready?"

"Yes!" I said. The team started to lift me up, pulling the rope hand over hand in a rhythmic motion until I was at the maximum height. The team supported my weight and held me firmly in place. Everything seemed as if it was moving in slow motion. Mark reiterated the purpose of the challenge was to let go. Let go of those things I had been holding onto that no longer serve any purpose in my life. It was as if he already knew my burdens, and how much I needed to release them.

"Whenever you are ready, Anni!" Mark shouted. I took a deep breath and instantly started crying.

Anyone who truly knows me knows I'm not a crier. I normally view crying as a sign of weakness, but for some reason, I couldn't hold it in. I had never cried in front of anyone except at funerals and that one time with Marcia. Nevertheless, here I was, like a fire hydrant opened up full blast, and I didn't care. There was no shame in showing the real me, the authentic and transparent me, for everyone to see.

God knew the desires of my heart, and I prayed for Him to free me of my burdens. Free me of the responsibility to hold everyone's life together. Free me from myself and the self-doubt and self-hate that often consumed me. Free me of my inability to save my brother from living in misery for seven years. Free me from the pain I had carried in my marriage, and open me up to new horizons and new experiences. Free me of the shame and guilt I retained as a result of marrying Dalton. Free me of the fear of leaving Dalton, and give me confidence to know I would make it out alive with my kids in tow. Prepare me for my new journey. I asked a lot of my new friend, God, as I dangled thirty-five feet in the air. *Help me to be renewed. Restored and fearless,* I prayed.

I let go of the rope that held me in place, and I threw my arms up in the air so I could experience the true free fall feeling without grasping any part of the rope. I no longer wanted to hold on to anything. That was my way of communicating to God that I let it all go, and I trusted that He would not let me fall. I had complete faith as I purposefully let go of all things, experiences, people and situations that no longer added value to my life. I swung freely back and forth like a pendulum. I was hysterical, sobbing uncontrollably. I was screaming to make sure I got everything out, and I left my burdens thirty-five feet above the earth for God to lift up and keep for himself.

I hung upside down, my limp body swinging carelessly, and Mark asked if I was all right. I quietly said, "Yes. Yes, I am." I was lowered to the ground and I noticed Michelle and Terri were crying. Most in the group empathized with me and wanted to show their support by giving me hugs, which felt good. I had convinced myself my entire life that I was not an emotional person, that I hated hugs and greetings with a kiss on top of the hug. That was never me. But, in that moment, that's exactly who I was. The emotional support and physical contact were exactly what I needed.

After each person had their turn, Mark gathered everyone into a group session where we talked about our experience and what the exercise meant for us. During my time to express myself, I talked about almost everything I had been holding onto and the pain those burdens had caused for so many years. (I left out the woes of my marriage because I wasn't comfortable talking about that in the group.) During the discussion, I was extremely tearful, and Terri was crying also, as she had never seen me so emotional. Michelle identified with me, as she too was the responsible one, and she expressed how burdensome that role can be.

This day, by far, had been the most liberating. I learned a great deal about myself on my last challenge at the resort. The day was emotional and draining, and I showed my vulnerable side for the first time in my life. Being encouraged and supported by the group that participated in the challenge was amazing. Resort mates, Amelia, Cindy and Steven, were with me in my first challenge with the tightrope, and having them support me again was awesome. They probably never realized how much I needed and appreciated their gift of strength. Complete strangers provided more than most of the people in my personal life. They were extraordinary people.

It felt liberating to show my vulnerability and talk openly about issues that had played a significant role in keeping me stuck in a rut emotionally, mentally and spiritually. This "aha moment" enabled me to release it all. Let it go. Let go of control (that's a hard one), and allow God to direct my path. I learned I was worthy and capable of great things in my life, and no longer responsible to hold everyone together. I had to follow my heart and do things that felt right for me in all facets of my life.

Chapter 17

I felt my friendship with Michelle and Terri had taken on new heights after sharing the powerful Swing and a Prayer exercise. I was proud of myself for going outside of my comfort zone, and it felt really good. I was excited about our experiences at the resort, the life lessons I had learned, and I was ready to get home and explore the world God was preparing for me. I even was ready to embrace my marriage in a new light. As we walked back from the challenge, Terri said, "How about we play a game tonight."

"I'm down, but what kind of game?" I asked.

Terri said, "Let's share what we think about each other." Michelle walked in silence and didn't chime in either way. My radar immediately started blaring and I thought to myself, *Hmm. That seems kind of weird.*

"Ok," I said hesitantly. Although a warning loomed in my head for a quick moment, I went back to feeling proud of myself and chose to reflect on my breakthrough instead of giving this "game" any thought.

My last day at Miraval was an awakening I had been searching for my whole life. I never felt so free, so unattached to the people and experiences that had plagued my life. I'd gained a new perspective on life, my marriage and myself as a mother, daughter, wife and friend. Life was not designed to be hard. God wants to take the reins and allow us to explore. We hold onto things that are toxic and fail to embrace the life God has etched in stone prior to our physical existence.

I had made a choice to marry Dalton, despite going against who I was as a person and the gut feeling I had that it was not the right thing to do. I can no longer use that decision to dictate which direction I was to travel in the future. I only had one life. Yes, I made a mistake, but it was time to figure out how to transform that mistake into a life lesson that propelled me forward.

Despite it all, Dalton needed me. He needed his children. If I allowed the past to separate us, what kind of person would that make me? I had to face the fact that we were forever going to be a family whether Dalton and I were married or separated. However, a change in our perspective, our attitude, and in our approach could mean all the difference in healing the wounds and moving forward. I didn't know if we could reconcile or not, but the Swing and a Prayer experience opened my eyes to the possibility of God renewing what He feels is salvageable. All I had to do was remain open and let God direct my steps.

I collected and packed my belongings in preparation for our departure the next day. After dinner, we planned to gather in Michelle's room for a final nightcap and play their silly game. I was exhausted. My emotions were raw after crying all morning, and my brain had worked overtime in self-reflection mode. I would have preferred to go back to my room and rest, and enjoy the peaceful comfort of my room one more evening before it was time to leave. I didn't feel comfortable with the game they wanted to play, and I didn't want it to ruin the high I was on from my challenge earlier in the day. Nevertheless, let the games begin.

I met Terri at her room, and we both walked over to

Michelle's since her room had the king size bed. We were in our pajamas, and I was at the head of the bed, while Michelle was on the side closest to the window. Terri lay horizontally across the foot of the bed, and was acting a bit aloof as the game was about to start. I got the impression I was being set up, as it seemed both ladies were aware of the game's intention.

"Terri, are you ready?" Michelle said.

"What exactly are we doing here?" I asked.

"Well, we'll take turns sharing our thoughts and feelings about each other regarding our friendship," Michelle said.

I was a bit perplexed about the reason this was necessary, especially after we had already shared so much of ourselves with each other. I thought I was as authentic as I could be earlier in the day. I left my soul totally exposed for all to see, pick over and analyze. What else was there for me to say? I really didn't know much about Michelle, because our "friendship" was non-existent outside of Terri, so I didn't really have anything to share. I kept wondering about the real purpose of this "game," but I didn't want to be a party-pooper.

Michelle seemed to be in charge, and she began by talking very highly of Terri. That was expected since they have been besties since high school, maybe earlier. Michelle shared her hope that Terri would open herself up to love in her life and stop being so picky. As Michelle talked, Terri sat back with her arms folded across her face as if she was embarrassed. Michelle concluded her thoughts by saying that she appreciated her lengthy friendship with Terri and how much she valued their relationship.

"Anni, it's your turn," Michelle said.

I was perplexed about where this was heading and what I should say. Although my friendship with Terri was never deep rooted in emotional stuff girlfriends share with one another, we were comfortable with where our friendship fell on the spectrum. We were not the kind of girlfriends who told each other everything. We did not call upon each other in time of need, with the exception of an airport pick up or drop off. Therefore, anything I said while playing this "game" was never going to be anything of substance.

"I'm a little confused on the rules and purpose of this game," I admitted, and neither of them responded. I started cautiously, because I was trying to determine the intent of this weird childish game. I shared how I appreciated Terri's research skills and how she was a pro at putting our vacations together by making sure our time together was packed with unique experiences. As I continued, I treaded lightly and tried to be positive about my comments, but I ended with one issue that was heavy on my heart.

Terri happened to be my son's godmother, and I was disappointed in her lack of involvement in Carter's life. Why would I give someone the awesome responsibility of the title of godmother to my child when we weren't even close friends? I think that decision was rooted in my belief that my relationship with Terri would grow, but it never did.

Once the subject was broached, I tried to explain how hurtful it was that Terri's only involvement with Carter was on his birthday and at Christmas. On both occasions, Terri would drop my son's gifts off by leaving them on our front porch and drive away. Half way down the block, she'd call or leave a message that Carter's gift was outside. Who does that to a kid, especially your godson? Is he not important enough to engage with, just for a few minutes, so he could at least put a name with the face? We both lived in the same area, minutes apart, and I didn't understand the problem. Instead of a gift, I'd prefer that Terri spend some quality time with Carter so they could get to know each other. I concluded my thoughts by saying it hurt me for my son's loss. I tried to word everything gently, albeit truthfully.

Michelle went off on me. "Terri is busy and so what if she leaves it at the door? At least she provides a gift. She does that for my daughter too," Michelle said dismissively. Michelle's daughter was also Terri's goddaughter. "Terri doesn't have time, but her intentions are good. Why would you have a problem with that?" Michelle was in full attack mode.

"What works for you doesn't work for me," I said defensively.

"Yeah, I don't have a husband to support me like you do, so I have to work and don't have time to come inside," Terri added.

Bingo! There it was - the reason for this game. Terri had an issue with me. The fact that I had a husband and she didn't, so she felt free to disrespect me? Now I understood their motive. They had something to say to me, but used this game as a ploy to say it. Why do women do that? If there is something that needs to be said, be an adult and say it. If we're friends, why do we have to plot and scheme against each other? I showed my vulnerable side and *this* is how I was repaid. Did they purposely wait until I had exposed my wounds to pour acid on my weeping sores?

This is a prime reason why many women are unable to engage in an authentic relationship with one another. Jealousy, resentment and egos are always at the forefront of a breakdown in friendship. After a few moments of silence, I concluded my thoughts by saying, "True and realistic relationships should have open constructive dialogue with one another instead of going into attack mode. We should respect each other enough to appreciate that the thoughts, feelings or opinions of others may be different than yours."

Instead of hearing the genuine need for my son to establish a healthy relationship with his godmother, these ladies seemed to focus on whatever agenda they had established prior to this trip. Apparently, me having a husband was a part of Terri's warped explanation as to why she could not spare ten minutes with my son. I should have gotten up and exited the room, but I stayed and waited for my flogging.

Rather than respond to my comment about true friends

respecting each other, Michelle quickly said, "Terri, you go next."

"Well, let's see..."Terri started. I knew my suspicion was correct. Terri had something on her mind and wanted to use a game to let it out. *How childish*, I thought. She began by mentioning an incident that had happened on Halloween five years earlier when Dalton and I took our kids trick or treating in her housing community and we ran into her. At the time, we joked about not seeing her around anymore, and now she was telling me that she felt "ambushed." Terri said since we made her feel uncomfortable, she purposely distanced herself from us for a while. She needed "a break from the friendship." We weren't even aware anything had happened and she needed a break? Dalton and I lack connections in our lives, so when we feel good about a relationship, especially one that involves our children, it is important to keep those people near and dear to our hearts. But it had become obvious that Terri had her own issues, especially if she felt we were a threat to her over expressing our concern for her not coming around to see us. This could have easily been resolved that same night if she had expressed how she felt.

I provided these points to Terri, but my explanation fell on deaf ears. Terri was eager to bring out my other "offenses." As Michelle sat quietly, Terri referenced the period of my brother's accident, confinement and subsequent death, saying she found it hard to be around me because I had become so angry. Michelle agreed and chimed in with, "You were too much to deal with."

My brother's accident was an unexpected tragedy. My family lived with enormous heartbreak for seven years as Owen withered away in a hospital bed. During that time, we also lost five key family members. It's a wonder I wasn't committed to a psych ward and strapped in a strait jacket.

"I'm sorry you both found it hard to be around me," I said. "But true friends would have been by my side supporting me along the way. My world had been turned upside down, and people of significance had been stripped away from me." I was fighting to hold back my tears and the urge to rip them both to shreds. Yes, you're damn right I was angry. Moreover, these two "friends" were never privy to the fact that my marriage was a mess on top of my other issues. I was carrying the world on my shoulders, and they were witness to that burden being released during our challenge this very day. How dare they confront me with such self-centered bull?

My suspicions were dead on. Michelle and Terri had been talking about me for a while. This "game" didn't come out of nowhere. Why did they choose to attack me on the one day I had let my guard down and exposed my vulnerability? Did they think I was going to be weak and unable to fight off their calculated maneuver? I had learned way too much about myself that day to allow someone with burdens and pains of their own to cast stones my way. There was no way Terri nor Michelle could ever understand the pain that took up residence in my heart as a result of my brother's accident. I endured unimaginable emotional turmoil and stress over the seven years of his paralysis prior to his death.

This moment showed me another side of Michelle and Terri. Who waits until a friend is completely emotionally naked to tear them down? Friends who no longer belong in your life, that's who. I didn't need friends who withheld their support and did not add value or benefit to my life, and would create a "game" rather than discuss a situation like an adult. Michelle wasn't a close friend anyway, but I realized I never truly knew Terri either. She always held me at arm's length and never discussed her personal life with me. Our relationship has forever changed because of what happened. There was no room in my life for people who were unwilling to care, and share, and be there to support each other during times of trouble.

Chapter 18

The morning of our departure was bittersweet. I was excited to get back home and tell Dalton about my trip and the experiences I had had. I was most eager to discuss how we could attempt to get our lives, family and marriage back on a positive track. I was going to miss the tranquility of Miraval, but I felt I had an arsenal of tools to help me along my new journey of self-discovery. My relationship with God was on the mend, and I had discovered the exact reason why I had left my job. God had a plan for my life, and He was setting things in motion.

As we met for breakfast prior to our airport transfer, I was being reclusive. I wasn't interested in being phony with Michelle and Terri, and small talk was the only thing I was offering. We loaded a small bus, and I overheard people sharing their Miraval experiences amongst each other. *Good*, I thought. It prevented me from engaging in conversation, and I could remain in solitude.

We arrived at the airport, checked in and went through the routine of boarding the plane. Michelle and I were assigned seats together. We were all tired, and sitting next to her wasn't a big deal. Prior to taxiing to the runway, we both texted our husbands to let them know we were on the plane. As we took off, I heard a click and a popping noise. I asked Michelle if she had heard the sound. "It's nothing," she said. "That was only the wheels coming up."

I had flown before and I knew it wasn't the wheels. Something seemed wrong. I watched out the window and noticed that we had circled the same place at least three times. I told Michelle, but she dismissed it and assured me everything was fine. About an hour into the flight, the pilot announced there was a problem with the landing gear and they were unable to complete the flight. Shortly thereafter, we were informed that the plane would be making an emergency landing in Phoenix, Arizona, and that we should prepare for a rough landing because the landing gear was not functioning properly.

I panicked. I was scared, and I wondered if this was the reason for my nervousness about going on this trip in the first place. I wasn't going to make it home. *Prepare for possible crash landing.* Did I hear that from the pilot, a flight attendant, or other passengers? All I could think of was what I'd seen on TV. The plane comes in for the landing, the landing gear buckles, and the plane skids, flips over, and burst into flames.

I turned on my phone and rang Dalton's cell number. "Hello?" he said.

"We might crash," I said. "I'm on the plane and the landing gear is not working and we have to prepare for a possible crash landing. I love you and the kids. Please tell my parents I love them too, just in case." There were no tears, but I was full of panic and anxiety. Did God get me to Miraval so I could make amends with Him before dying? Was this His way of saving my soul before He took me to be with Him? Michelle kept assuring me we were going to be fine.

The plane made its approach and I recall bracing myself the way the flight attendants instructed. Luckily, we landed perfectly fine and the landing gear didn't malfunction as they had anticipated. I closed my eyes and thanked God for sparing my life. I started making promises; you know, the ones you make when God spares your life?

As with most unexpected travel mishaps, there was a mad dash to rebook flights. Long lines were already formed when we exited the plane, and chaos ensued. *There goes my tranquility.* Michelle, Terri and I managed to get on the same flight in our attempt to get home, which left late in the evening and was expected to arrive the next morning. So now, I was forced to act like nothing was wrong for the next several hours. While we waited in the airport, we ate, read silently and sat around for most of the day and into the evening. The layover felt like an eternity, but we were finally on our way home. The three of us were seated together, but thankfully, it was an overnight flight so there was little interaction between us.

We arrived close to 7:00 am the next morning. As the plane touched down, I called Dalton to let him know we had arrived safely and that Terri's mother was picking us up from the airport.

"Ok," he said in a dry tone, not offering anything else to the conversation.

What's his problem!? I was way too tired to entertain whatever was going on with him. I said, "Ok," and hung up.

Terri's mother was there to meet us, and since Terri and I live in the same town, Michelle was dropped off first. There were no warm hugs, but we maintained a sense of courtesy to each other. We pulled up to my house and the front door was open, with our dog, Kaiser, standing up inside the screen door when he saw the car enter the driveway. That was strange. I had texted Dalton to alert him that I was close, and I expected him to be waiting in the doorway. He always waited for me, even when I returned home after a night out. The only one waiting for me this time was Kaiser.

I removed my luggage from the trunk and waved goodbye

to Terri and her mother. I felt a familiar heaviness as I rolled my luggage up the driveway between our two parked cars. I approached the front door, opened the screen, and dragged my luggage inside. Kaiser was so excited, and I could barely get into the house. His short stubby tailed swished wildly, and I greeted him in my doggy high-pitched voice and a loving pat on his head. "Hello?" I called out.

"Yeah!" Dalton called from the kitchen.

Oh, here we go! I went into the kitchen, and he was standing with his back to me, making his breakfast before work. It took him a few seconds to turn around, and in that instant, I was right back where I started. The heavy feeling I had had in the driveway had been a warning.

I pushed the feeling of dread aside and tried to adopt the new life perspective I had learned, and maintain the happy memories from my trip. I embraced him, but he felt cold... distant. I tried to ignore the negative energy he was emitting and stay positive, but it was unbearable.

"What's wrong?" I asked.

"Nothing. Trying to get myself ready for work," he said. I had been away for five days, on a life changing adventure, and I walked right back into the life I thought I had left thirty-five feet in the air on the Swing and a Prayer Challenge. My excitement turned into disappointment. He was upset, but I had no idea why. I was tired and hungry and had no energy for what was happening in that moment. I rambled a bit about my trip and highlighted a few things I experienced. Dalton, uninterested, pretended to listen as he prepped for work.

I stayed in the kitchen, trying unsuccessfully to engage Dalton in conversation before he left for work. Perhaps he was snubbing me because he was envious of my time away and didn't want to hear about it when he had to go to work, so I gave the exchange little thought. I was happy to be home and excited to be in my own bed and sleep soundly without fear of something crawling around me. Dalton left for work, and I quickly prepped to crawl into bed. As my head hit the pillow, I briefly wondered what was going on with Dalton. Before I knew it, I was sound asleep.

Chapter 19

For the first few weeks of being home, I tried my best to maintain my excitement and the positive outlook I'd gained from my trip. The kids were still away at my parents, and Dalton and I had the remainder of the summer to enjoy our childfree environment. However, something was different. Dalton was different. He would come home from work, grab a snack, hit the couch and take a nap. He didn't seem interested in talking, sharing my newfound enthusiasm for life or my rekindled relationship with God. I was going to church alone as Dalton had no interest in joining me, despite my requests that he go with me. He was in his own world, and I had no idea why.

I recognized that we had marital issues that had loomed over us since the day we said our I-do's, but I was fine when I got back from Miraval. I felt that I had a new lease on life, only to be sucked right back to the life I had been desperately trying to escape. One day I walked in on a conversation Dalton was having on the phone with his birth sister, Nicole. He kept repeating, "I don't know," which was obviously the code that I was listening.

The next day, Nicole called me. I was a bit surprised, considering his family never called me. We engaged in small talk for a few minutes, and then she expressed concern about Dalton. I told her I honestly had no clue what was going on with him and shared that he had been acting strange ever since I returned from my trip. Nicole said that Dalton was considering leaving the marriage. "What marriage," I asked? "We have not had a 'marriage' since three months *before* our vows, so how could he leave something we both were never fully engaged in?"

There was silence on the phone, as if my response took Nicole by surprise. I continued telling Nicole who her brother really was, since no one knew the authentic Dalton or what I had been through before or after we got married. I acknowledged that Dalton was loving, kind, physically protective and everyone adored him, including myself. Like many people, he had emotional baggage, but Dalton had varying complexities to his unique story. He had failed to share those details with Nicole, so she was missing some important information about my relationship with Dalton that she wasn't taking into consideration. I remembered thinking, *Dalton's got a lot of nerve saying* he *wants to leave after all I've been through with this man.* I told Nicole, "He has my permission to leave because I can no longer rescue him from himself. It's time to rescue myself."

Dalton's issues over his adoption, his mother and father, his insecurities and the necessity for me to treat him like a child were getting to be way too much for me to deal with. I deserved to have a life much better than the one I'd been enduring. I realized life couldn't always be sunshine and a bed of roses, but when was I ever going to enjoy some happiness without someone coming along to rob me of my joy and sanity? As my conversation ended, Dalton walked in.

"I just got off the phone with Nicole," I said.

"Oh yeah," he said with a nonchalant look on his face.

"So, what's going on?" I asked.

"Nothing," he quipped.

"Something," I said. Talking to Dalton was like pulling teeth. In order for him to open up, I had to ask him a million questions to get to the point, and today I didn't feel like playing the game. "So you want to leave?"

"I'm thinking about it," he said.

"Ok. Let me know when you decide what you want to do," I stated and walked away. Our marriage had been difficult, to say the least. We had endured turmoil from every spectrum imaginable, and I didn't have the strength to continue trying to get answers from Dalton. At this point, I didn't care if there was someone else he was interested in, or if he had already been unfaithful. I didn't care anymore. I was burdened with an unbelievable amount of people's crap, and I refused to continue to carry any of it. *I'm doing me.*

I occupied the remainder of the summer with walks in the park, relaxation and reading. Against my better judgement, I started hanging out with Terri and Michelle. They were a convenient escape and a distraction until my kids returned from their summer with my parents. Despite what had taken place at Miraval, they invited me out and I needed a diversion, so I accepted their invitations. I really didn't want to be with them, but it was better than being alone.

Chapter 20

Once the kids returned home and were settled in school, I finally started to dedicate my full attention to my small business. This was a welcomed distraction, and it couldn't have come at a more perfect time with the distance between Dalton and me growing daily. Although I had no clue what the foundation of this business was going to be, I did have an idea of what I wanted to offer. As a licensed Social Worker, throughout my career I had had to delve into background stories, and I was always intrigued by the family dynamics from which people emerge. How did they get where they were in life? What negative/positive influences changed the course of their life? How much do people really know about their family circle?

I found that most family members were not even aware of their relatives' life stories until they read it in an obituary. Why do we wait to find out who a person truly is until they are dead? It's too late to have a conversation about any discoveries that are made because the person is now deceased. I wanted my business to address those questions by giving a voice to people's backstories while they are alive.

My original idea was an online storybook or maybe a computerized diary. I was never a fan of sharing personal information online, but I was informed that everything today centers around the internet. I did the necessary research, developed a business plan, and organized focus groups to get started. I wrote down every facet of the business structure and what I needed to accomplish my vision, which grew to include identifying my life goals.

It was as if God started speaking to me again. *You are destined for greatness. There is a plan for your life. There is something major you must do.* I soon realized that not only was I writing my business goals, I was creating objectives for an author, an advocate, and a speaker. Given my shy tendencies and fear of public speaking, it was strange to imagine myself being an author or orator. I had nothing important to say or talk about, and I never dreamed for a second that anyone would be interested in my thoughts. I found it hilarious and believed my mind was playing tricks on me. However, advocacy was right up my alley, and correcting a wrong was my forte. Fighting injustice and treating people with kindness and respect was my persona. I recognized my strengths *and* my weaknesses, and I knew what fit and what didn't. Finding my thoughts drifting on too many things at one time, I decided to ignore the ideas that were out of my comfort zone for now.

Most entrepreneurs will testify that starting a business is exciting, but it also makes you want to pull your hair out! Nothing was working out right. The web developer I had hired was not meeting the deadlines we had discussed and proved unable to deliver the product and services that had been outlined. At the time, I saw this as a major setback. Maybe I wasn't cut out to be an entrepreneur. Many days I felt like I was pulled backward more often than I moved forward. In this arena, only the strong survive. You are the only one accountable for deadlines, results, plans and goals. There is no one to push you or help you. With the weight of my marriage and the quicksand up to my knees, I gave up. I had always been successful at everything. I had never failed in my professional life. This setback played like a broken record in my head. *You can't succeed. You can't succeed. Go get yourself a regular job.*

The encouragement I gained from my Miraval experience was slowly slipping from my grasp. Oprah's shows on OWN, which had previously giving me such strength, were no longer pushing me forward toward achieving the success I wanted. Neither the leadership trainings I attended nor the empowerment conferences were doing anything to get me unstuck. I was beyond the "You can do it! Capture your success! Let's Go!" rhetoric I had heard at those motivational seminars. What do you do when those mantras no longer motivate you beyond the exit door of the seminar? I had truly believed I was free from the bondage, and the heaviness I carried was slowly being unraveled to reveal a much stronger me. A more resilient me. I tried to push through and hold on to the promises I believed God had for me, but I was in a weakened state. I felt beaten down. I wasn't accustomed to being a failure at anything. Well, my marriage was failing, but that wasn't on me alone.

My ego placed me back into a box to "protect" me from the things I feared. Building this business made me afraid, and I found myself in a stagnant routine. Paralyzed emotionally, physically exhausted and unbalanced. How could I be stuck? My mind told me I couldn't achieve my goals because I was not talented enough, worthy enough, and too scared to act.

I should have known better than to believe that. I graduated from a prestigious university, and I know I am proficient. I worked diligently to earn the director's position at the senior citizen health program. Despite never having any supervisory experience, with a simple vision and believing I was capable of the job, I was a success. I have always been confident in my abilities, my talents, my wisdom and myself. Fear had no place in my life. Fear is not positive. Fear can't help me do anything. Fear does not get me where I need to be. Fear suffocates dreams and clouds vision. Fear had no place for where I was going. Why had these negative thoughts resurfaced? "What am I missing here, God?" I asked aloud. I decided to take a step back and slow myself down.

I enjoyed staying home and taking life as it came, but I had become consumed with my negative thoughts. I was utterly confused and didn't know what to do. Having no job to go to, once my household responsibilities were met, I watched TV. I relied heavily on OWN, The Oprah Winfrey Network, to help sustain me with its inspiring broadcast of shows. I was addicted to *Iyanla: Fix My Life, Super Soul Sunday,* and *Life Class,* with experts sharing their personal life struggles and words of inspiration. I had my journal ready to jot down all the recommendations and lessons offered, hoping to get my life in gear.

My obsession with OWN was crazy. Oprah became a goddess to me. I hung on her every word and desperately tried to apply her wisdom to my circumstances. Everything personally and professionally had become an enormous struggle for me. Dalton remained in a fog and offered little support, and the demands of motherhood were once again overwhelming me. I wasn't happy, but why? *Why am I grasping the negativity that is meant to destroy me? I'm holding on to a sinking ship, willing to drown rather than fight for life.*

Chapter 21

Dalton had finally decided to stay in the marriage, but I didn't know if that was a good or bad thing. Part of me yearned that everything wrong would be righted, miraculously fixed, and we would be happy. Another part of me wanted him to go. I wanted a fresh start without him. A do-over at life. From the beginning, our marriage had been stress-filled, and there was enough resentment to fill a thousand potholes. We tried to move forward, pretending that nothing was wrong.

I became a stay-at-home mom once again, where I cooked and cleaned and waited for everyone to return home from work and school. We started sitting at the dinner table again, in a renewed effort to be a normal family. Although we did not have the best role models, we were attempting to do things differently with our kids. Consciously, we knew our marriage was a mess, but subconsciously, we were trying to stop our kids from repeating the same patterns in their future relationships. Dalton and I developed an unspoken truce, and we seemed content with each other. Everyone was enjoying me staying home except me. I was falling into the domestic role I despised. Don't get me wrong. I was enjoying being there for my family, but I was losing myself in loads of daily laundry, errands, daytime TV, and preparing endless meals. Where did I fit in the equation? I was meeting everyone's needs except my own.

I started getting out of the house by attending various entrepreneurial networking events throughout the greater NYC area and I soon learned a terrible truth about networking. No one cares about your business. Networking is a cliché. Either you're in or you're out. No one was interested in learning about my business, because everyone was busy pushing their own concept or agenda. Partnership offers were thrown around, but the unspoken intention was for you to invest in them and send referrals their way.

It was hard for me to play the game, but I tried. I would attend meetings, stand up and present my business concept to the masses, sit down, and the next person would go. Very few people were truly interested in getting to know anyone outside their inner circles, let alone hearing about new ideas. Some attendees used the free time away from work to relax. They threw brochures, note pads, pens and other promotional items on a table, sat back and socialized without uttering a word about why they were there. This sounds like I was bitter that no one would buy into my concept, but that's not the case at all. Everyone believed my service was needed, but I had a hard time sealing the deal.

My problem was that I wasn't a salesperson. I wasn't pushy, and I didn't make a big enough impression to be convincing. I would share information, and that would be it. Meeting after meeting, conference after conference, I ended up with the same results, which was nothing. No sales. No interest in moving past go. Some helpful people would share information on other networking groups and suggested other avenues to explore, but things weren't moving fast enough, if at all. *What's wrong with me? Why can't I get this done?* I was falling into a depression. I was so hard on myself. I wanted to give up. I had quit my job with no plan in place. *Now look where you are,* I thought. *They're all going to laugh at you for sure.* "God what am I doing!" I yelled!

I tried to renew my enthusiasm by listening to motivational speakers on YouTube. I reviewed my Oprah and *Deepak Chopra 21 Day Meditation Challenges,* watched *Oprah's Master Class* over and over. I read books Oprah recommended and looked over my journal with the inspiring quotes I had picked up along the way, to no avail. I was stuck yet again. I seemed to be repeating a cycle throughout this journey. I'd get inspired, attempt to move forward, and fall backward again.

I know success. I've been successful. What the heck had happened to me? I was going around and around on life's rollercoaster, and one day I got an email about Oprah's *The Life You Want* Tour. Maybe *this* is what I need, I told myself. I need a fresh start and this is it! I will hear firsthand how others overcame fear, failure and obstacles. I'm so there!

Going to my computer, I researched seats and pricing options. "Jeez, these tickets are expensive and I'm unemployed," I told myself. There was a VIP ticket that included a meeting with Oprah in a smaller, more intimate setting, but those tickets were way too expensive. However, I made sure I selected seats close to the stage so I could take everything in. I really believed this experience was going to change my life for the better and pull me out of the quicksand I'd been stuck in for a while.

I purchased two tickets, even though I didn't know who I was going to take with me. I thought about Terri, but that Miraval experience lingered in my mind. *I'll take Dalton,* I thought. But he can be so blasé and unimpressed about things, and I wanted to experience this tour with excitement. I was often indifferent about things too, so I needed someone who could balance that out, and Dalton was not the person to do that. However, I felt I had to let him know I was going, so I told him that I had purchased the tickets.

Outside of the shock of how much the tickets cost, to my surprise, he wanted to go. He had grown tired of me choosing to vacation alone and hanging out with Terri and Michelle. He seemed eager to go, and I told him I needed him to be excited since this wasn't an ordinary vacation. This was important! We both suffered with shyness, but there would be no bashfulness allowed. I wanted to be free of drama and not worry about anything. He agreed to my terms. Although there were tour dates throughout the U.S., I chose Washington, D.C. because that was around my birthday weekend. What a way to spend my birthday!

Chapter 22

My mom traveled to New York to watch the kids for the weekend. Dalton and I drove to D.C., and it was fantastic. We were relaxed and connected for the first time in a long while. It reminded me of times that we were close, without a care in the world, and that made for an awesome trip. Once getting to the Hyatt Hotel in downtown D.C., we settled down. The Verizon Center, with Oprah somewhere inside, was within walking distance.

As we anticipated the first round of events, I was excited. I was finally going to see my idol in the flesh. I found myself thinking I wanted to be someone else. I didn't want to be the shy Anni I had been all my life. The Anni who was uncomfortable speaking in public or being seen. I have a strong personality, but most people rarely get to see that side of me. I wanted to be free, to express myself without judgment from others. I wanted to talk to strangers and engage in the festivities without hesitation or overthinking. I wanted to enjoy my husband's presence without any negative thoughts about how uncomfortable he was at this event or the pitfalls of our marriage. I didn't want to be annoyed with the limiting thoughts that had been looming in my psyche over the past few months. I didn't want the failed attempts of my business coming to mind, or any of the burdens I'd carried. I wanted to be in my own world, having my once-in-a-lifetime experience with the woman who had convinced me to quit my job and seek the life I deserved.

In the Verizon Center there were stations with books, bags, tee-shirts, and a variety of things Oprah and her affiliated sponsors had on sale. There were big name vendors like Ikea and Toyota that had interactive stations. There was a jam session where a live DJ played the latest hits and a break out dance party going on. There was an overall positivity about everything, and excitement was in the air.

Dalton felt out of place among the sea of woman. We began to explore everything, and it wasn't long before he expressed regret in coming with me. I reminded him of the terms he had agreed to, and I asked him not to ruin the experience for me and be happy for me because I was happy. This experience was something I desperately needed. I told him we both needed this excitement in our life, and hopefully, whatever we learn during this event would aid us in moving forward in our lives, in our marriage, and guide us as parents. (Ok, that's a lot of pressure on the presenters, but I could dream.) Agreeing to fight through his discomfort, Dalton promised to stay positive and accept whatever happened. As we walked around, Dalton swore to show his support for any other guys he saw by giving them a high-five. That was his way to acknowledge the men who had been dragged there by their significant other. A show of solidarity. Not many men were present, but there were a few that shared a high-five with Dalton.

The first night was electrifying. The stadium was filled to capacity, and since we were about nine rows from the front, there was a clear view of the stage. Music flowed throughout the stadium, and it was as if people were bursting at the seams to let their souls free. The lights dimmed and Oprah appeared on the stage, looking stunning in a red formal floor length gown. *I should have paid the extra money for the VIP ticket to meet her,* I thought. Oprah talked about living out your purpose, and she set the foundation for what we should expect the next day. Every guest was given a bracelet that lit up with such a beautiful array of colors that they illuminated the entire stadium. This was going to be an incredible birthday. Even Dalton was filled with excitement. We were given a workbook and a VIP bag with extra goodies because even though we had not purchased the VIP tickets we were seated in that section.

After Oprah's welcome to the tour that Friday evening, we went to explore the rest of the festivities. As we walked and explored the exhibits and sponsored areas, we found the *O Magazine* lounge. Not knowing what the exhibit was about, we got in the line when we noticed there was buzz that Gayle King was there greeting people. We got closer to the doorway and made our way inside the lounge, and we heard an announcement that we could meet Gayle King and have a photo taken with her if we were interested in purchasing a subscription to *O, The Oprah Magazine,* often simply called *O.* We were unsure if we should stay because the tickets to the event were not cheap and we didn't want to be tempted to spend more money. Standing in the midst of the excitement in the room, we stayed in line to see what was going on.

A woman came up to us and asked us why we had come to the event. We didn't know if she worked there or was making small talk, but she introduced herself as Lucy. Dalton told her that we had traveled from New York to D.C. in honor of my birthday. Lucy told us that the Oprah tour was also going to New Jersey and that would have been closer. Dalton explained that we wanted to make a weekend getaway out of the celebration. Lucy asked Dalton how he felt to be at the tour with all these women, and he responded by saying he wanted to meet the person (Oprah) responsible for convincing his wife to leave her job. She looked at me and said, "Really?"

I explained that, for years, I had a nagging feeling to leave my job, but it wasn't until I watched *Oprah's Master Class* that I was convinced to get moving. Oprah talked about being in flow and listening to that small voice that is deep down inside that will guide us through life. Never had anyone been able to provide a description of what I was feeling. The tugging of my soul, to move in one direction over another, was all so new to me, but Oprah described it to a tee. Lucy appeared surprised at my candor, but before she could say anything else, Gayle King appeared in the room.

Gayle was a lot taller than I had imagined. She seemed fun to be around, and she smiled and was friendly as she made her way through the line meeting and greeting guests. Lucy said she was going to see if she could get Gayle to come over and speak to us. What? Dalton and I looked at each other in amazement. We couldn't believe we were going to be meeting Gayle King, Oprah's BFF!

Lucy approached Gayle, who was talking with a few women ahead of us in the line. She mouthed a few words and pointed in our direction. "Here she comes!" Dalton said. Gayle made her way to the people directly in front of us, and asked Lucy, "Them?" Gayle didn't wait for Lucy's response, and she started talking to the women directly in front of us! *Oh no!* Humble, and not wanting to make a fuss, we stayed quiet and observed Gayle engage with the group. With great disappointment, we watched Gayle skip right over us and head to a group behind us. Dalton looked over at Lucy as if to say, "Hey, please get Gayle to come back." Lucy shrugged her shoulders, as if she had done her best and didn't want to annoy Gayle.

Dalton went into action and animated a begging motion for Lucy, and a few minutes later, she graciously directed Gayle back to us. *Thank you, Lord,* I thought. Gayle was upbeat, positive, and definitely a people person. Dalton and I were so excited and totally amazed that she was standing in front of us and we were talking. Gayle asked us our names and what had brought us to the tour. Dalton took charge of the conversation and repeated everything he had said to Lucy. Gayle got a kick out of Dalton claiming Oprah was responsible for me quitting my job. She looked at me and said, "What? You quit your job? Why?" I told Gayle how I watched *Oprah's Master Class* and how I learned so much about myself, and finally understood the quiet still voice I had been hearing for years.

Gayle asked for the spelling of our names. "A-N-N-I," I said. "D-A-L-T-O-N," Dalton said.

Gayle looked at the names she had written and asked, "Anni and Dalton?"

"Yes, that's correct," Dalton said.

"Ok," she said, and she started jotting down some things in a little notebook she had with her.

What's happening?

Gayle commented on how happy she was to see Dalton support me in such a big way. The more we talked, the more she wrote down. Gayle then explained the benefits of O's Circle of Friends, which is a club that provides perks and privileges in connection to the world of Oprah Winfrey and includes a subscription to *O, The Oprah Magazine*. She asked if we were interested, and I told her we really shouldn't because we'd already spent too much, and how I was truly grateful for the trip itself. In front of Gayle, Dalton asked me, "Are you sure? We can get it." Gayle said, "You will get a picture with me and you'll get bumped to the front of the line," she sang with the same big smile she offers up to Charlie Rose on *CBS This Morning*. I graciously declined, not wanting to add any more expense to the weekend.

Gayle thanked us for coming to the tour and moved on towards the back of the line. Dalton said, "Listen, don't worry about the money. This is a time to celebrate. Not to be shy, remember? Not hold anything back. No regrets." He reminded me of the freedom I desired from coming here, and he insisted we get the subscription. I reluctantly agreed. "Gayle, Gayle, Gayle!" Dalton yelled.

"What are you doing," I said. "You can't call after Gayle like that."

"Yes, Dalton!" Gayle replied and our eyes sprung wide open. Was this happening? Was Gayle actually answering my husband's shouts? Yes. Yes she was!

Gayle walked back to us and Dalton said, "We'll get the subscription!"

Gayle immediately removed us from the line and ordered Dalton to pull out his cell phone and take a picture of me with her. She told us to switch places so Dalton could also take a picture, but Dalton declined. He's not really a star struck person, but I think he was being a little shy and didn't want to seem like a groupie. Gayle took me by my hand as Dalton followed us to a young man who provided us with payment directions and a card verifying our subscription order. Gayle thanked us once again and off she went to work the rest of the line.

I had my *O* cover page photo taken with Oprah (on green screen that is), and I was on cloud nine! We tried to absorb what had happened, and we ran into Lucy, the person who had orchestrated the events of our memorable experience. We thanked her so much that she was probably thinking we were a little weird. Dalton and I were the type of people that are genuinely thankful for any acts of kindness shown to us. Once we got back to the hotel that evening, I studied the itinerary like the Bible, because I didn't want to miss anything.

Chapter 23

We got up on Saturday and rushed to eat breakfast and get to the activities on time. As Dalton and I walked toward the venue hand and hand, we both felt something magical in the air, but we didn't quite know what. Maybe it was that we were actually holding hands. We hadn't done that in a long time. We felt weightless and excited about the day's full agenda.

We entered The Verizon Center, made our way to our seats, and noticed the place was packed more so than the day before! There were very few men to be seen, but the environment was so electrical we felt the energy deep down in our souls. Like many others, Dalton and I took selfies and pictures near the stage, with the huge backdrop displaying the thousands of tweets happening throughout the arena. DJ Kiss's music filled the atmosphere with amazing sounds, and people broke loose, dancing in the aisles, in their seats, on the stairs, and everywhere in between.

When we took our seats and the house lights dimmed, bracelets that had been given to each participant began to light up and illuminate an array of colors as Oprah took the stage. She belted out a huge welcome and excited the crowd even more. After a few words, Oprah asked, "Where's Dalton from New Jersey?"

My eyebrows rose in astonishment, and I whispered to Dalton, "Is she talking to you?" He quickly waved me off, as if to say no.

"Dal-Ton! Where are you Dal-Ton?" she repeated in a sexy Eartha Kitt voice.

I told Dalton, "That's you! That's us!" I stood up and yelled, "Here we are Oprah!" I threw my shyness out the window. Dalton was frozen to his seat. Oprah turned in our direction and put her hand to her forehead, blocking the bright lights. Peering into the crowd, she said, "Stand up!"

I shouted to Dalton, "Oprah's talking to you! You have to stand up!" I didn't want to lose this moment, and I shouted toward the stage, "We're right here Oprah! We're from New York." Reluctantly, Dalton stood up and Oprah began to have a full-fledged conversation with him.

"From New York? Why are you in D.C. if you're from New York?" she asked. Before we could answer, Oprah said that Gayle had been talking about us last night, telling her about our meeting in the *O Magazine* room. Dalton began to engage in a one-on-one conversation with Oprah, just like they were old friends! Dalton was explaining why we were there, initially unaware that there was a camera crew standing in front of him with a microphone, recording the exchange. All of a sudden, Dalton looked up and saw our faces plastered over every single Jumbo Tron in the arena. He pushed the microphone away and sat down, rendered speechless.

Oprah continued talking and joking with Dalton, and she said, "Oh, Dalton, you're going to have a great night tonight for bringing Anni here." Feeling totally embarrassed, Dalton completely shut down. I tried my best to get him to stand up, but he was done. I pulled on him, yanked on his clothes and kept begging, "Please get up," but he was in a daze. Oprah thanked us for coming and moved on to give another guest the thrill of their life.

I sat down, regaining my composure, while Dalton stared forward quietly for a brief moment. He later explained the encounter as if Oprah's soul and his soul were magnetized. He recalled feeling a rush of heat throughout his body as if something had been jump started. I'd never known Dalton to be star-struck, but Oprah was not your normal celebrity. She had something special within her, as Dalton had now realized for himself. We knew when we were walking over to the venue that something magical was in store. Never in a million years would we have expected Oprah to be speaking directly to us in an arena full of thousands of people. Dalton and I are shy, and don't mind blending in with the wallpaper to avoid standing out, but this felt good. Better than good, this felt amazing. Something within us felt awake and alive, and we wanted to relish in "it" for as long as we could.

During the lunch break, we went to retrieve our pre-ordered lunch boxes, and we were flooded with congratulations and conversations from everyone we encountered. People called out to Dalton by name and said "Happy Anniversary" to us, and although we were celebrating my *birthday*, we didn't mind one bit. We felt on top of the world. We are such humble people, but I have to admit, the attention felt incredible. I recall feeling so happy for Dalton. For once in his life, he was being acknowledged and allowing people to shower him with pleasantries. His humility ran deep and he found it uncomfortable to stand out. I could see the pride rise up in him, as well as his confidence. Being who we are, we felt it necessary to show our gratitude to the woman who had introduced us to Gayle.

During another break, we made our way back to the *O Magazine* lounge. We were able to avoid the long lines, since we had already ordered a subscription. We entered the room and approached Gayle, who was amongst the crowd. When she saw us she shouted, "Dalton and Anni!" She gave us both a big hug. I couldn't believe she remembered our names and she treated us like friends she had known for years. She was so happy for us that Oprah had talked to us and we got the biggest shout-out of our lives.

Dalton told Gayle that the encounter was magical and how thankful we were that she had talked to Oprah and made it happen. Gayle was amazed that we came back to the lounge to find her. She exclaimed, "You came back to say thank you?" She gave us a hug again, and onlookers were wondering, "Who are these people?" Gayle made us feel important. Made us feel special, and we would never forget that feeling. As Gayle hugged us goodbye, she grasped Dalton's arm and said, "Ooh Dalton! We love Dalton, don't we, ladies?" And all the women in the line yelled out, "Yes!"

"Would it be rude to ask him to take his shirt off, Anni?" Gayle asked with a sly smile.

Jokingly, I said, "Go ahead, Dalton. Take your shirt off!" Not to pimp out my husband, but hey, it was Gayle. Although Dalton acted as if he was going to remove his shirt, he did not.

We searched the crowd for Lucy, the woman who was the catalyst in the chain of events that gave us the time of our lives. We felt such gratitude that we were practically floating on air.

"There she is!" I said. Dalton and I embraced Lucy with open arms and thanked her with all our hearts. We shared with her that we had a feeling something magical was going to happen, and we were truly grateful for God directing her to us. She was a true Godsend to initiate this once-in-a-lifetime experience. We were filled with love and happiness, and we wanted to hug Lucy again and again. I supposed that would have been really weird, so we tried to contain the "high" we were on and act normal.

As we traveled home, we couldn't help but be amazed at the sequence of events. If Lucy hadn't talked to us, we wouldn't have encountered Gayle, and Gayle wouldn't have spoken to Oprah, and Oprah would not have called us out. Did Lucy work with Gayle or Oprah? We couldn't tell if she was a part of the tour or not, but I started googling her name on the ride home. We had to send her a "Thank you" card, or a letter, or something to express our gratitude. I didn't know Lucy's last name, but for some reason I went to Google Images. Maybe, just maybe, I would see a picture and place the face with a full name.

The power of the internet is fierce. There she was! "I got a picture of Lucy, Dalton!" I exclaimed as he was driving.

"What's her full name? Does she work with Gayle?" he asked.

"Omg!" I cried with excitement.

"What?" Dalton said, trying to be patient.

"Lucy is the Editor-in-Chief of *O!*" I said.

"Are you serious?" Dalton replied.

"Yes!" I said. Oh my goodness. We had actually been talking to the Editor-In-Chief of Oprah's magazine, and we had had no clue. This was beyond amazing. God had lined up some incredible people to make this experience awesome. I had to acknowledge the fact that none of this would have happened if I had taken anyone other than Dalton with me on this trip. Dalton was the one that lured Lucy over to us, because he caught her attention as being one of a few men in the place.

Dalton might carry some heavy baggage, but his spirit is so big and inviting that he was able to connect with Gayle and Oprah in a way that I couldn't. I'm a good person, but there is something extra special about Dalton that is undeniable. He is like a light that shines ever so brightly and is able to attract others. Although he has yet to discover his talent of having a spiritual influence on people, I've always believed he has the ability within him.

Chapter 24

We returned home with such joy, excitement and readiness to take on new challenges. With a new and improved website, I went back into the networking world with a brighter perspective to market my business. I did my best to block out any obstacles that had previously presented themselves and move forward with the positive mindset Oprah and the other presenters talked about on the *Live Your Life* Tour. I reviewed my notes to incorporate everything that was discussed, hoping that information would help turn me into the successful woman I was used to being.

I couldn't seem to shake a familiar feeling that something wasn't quite right. But what? I had changed my mindset. My outlook on life was bigger. I was repeating my mantras. I was doing my Oprah and Deepak meditations. I was creating my goals for success. I was reaching out to people and not letting my shyness take control. So what was the problem here? I was still riding the high of the tour but falling flat at the same time. *Push through it, Anni,* I told myself repeatedly. *You can do this!* Self-motivation had become my banner. If I couldn't motivate myself, no one else was going to do it.

After a month of trying to forge ahead in my business, the administrator from the job I had resigned from called me with an opportunity as a consultant in another senior health care program. She wanted me to review the operations and make recommendations regarding how to get the program on a successful track. *Wow*, I thought. *This is the break I've been looking for.* This was something to get me out the house a few hours each week and regain a feeling of accomplishment, not to mention earning a few extra bucks.

This offer couldn't have come at a better time. I was back at it! Leadership was always my comfort zone. Operational analysis and strategic planning was second nature to me, and I was at ease in my new position. This brought back my familiar feeling of success, and it felt so good. Getting dressed, putting on those heels and heading off to work to do what I did best was an amazing feeling. I loved to help people and develop staff to work efficiently. I was good at making people feel like they mattered and that they are important to the success of their department regardless of their position.

I loved the staff and always enjoyed working with Ms. Michaels, my administrator. I felt like I was living for a purpose, and Ms. Michaels came knocking at the right time. I worked as a consultant for almost a year. The facility had begun to restructure by bringing on a new CEO, and I decided to move on. Besides, I was more interested in getting back to business ownership, so I helped the administrator secure a full time director and assisted with the training. Shortly after deciding not to continue with the consultant job, I found myself regretting it because the work was meaningful for me. Helping senior citizens and their families and being a strong advocate for employees filled my soul.

After leaving the consultant job, I called a friend who I had always admired. Gabriel owned many successful businesses, and I was hoping he would consider mentoring me and help me learn to be successful in my own business. I met with

Gabriel to go over my business plan, strategies, and goals, and he briefly looked at my ideas.

"No one is going to be interested in this business. I wouldn't want your services, and I couldn't imagine anyone else would either," Gabriel said matter-of-factly.

I was floored at his blunt opinion, and my self-esteem instantly flew out the window. I explained my reasons for starting the business with the hope he would sympathize with my intentions, but he never got it. In retrospect, I could see he had an ulterior motive.

"Do you have any other questions you'd like to ask me about this business of yours?"

"No," I said hopelessly.

"Ok, good. Let's get to the matter at hand," Gabriel proclaimed. "I need a director to restructure the senior program."

"I'm no longer doing that kind of work, but if you're looking for me to be a consultant and oversee your current director I can do that," I said confidently.

"I don't want a consultant," Gabriel explained. "I need someone to do the work. I already know what's needed. I need you to duplicate the success you had at your previous job." I was feeling low, but I tried to hide my frustration as he took me on a tour of the facility. "So, what do you think?"

"I don't know," I said as I went through everything in my mind.

I really didn't want to be responsible for the day-to-day operations, and I wasn't looking to be tied down to a full time job. I was escorted back to the conference room where Gabriel said, "Name your price."

What? No one had ever said that to me. It was certainly an ego booster, but it was not what I wanted to do. Everything was thrown at me to convince me to take the offer. Bonuses, opportunities in other areas, flexible schedule with no set hours as long as the work was done. Basically, I would have carte blanche.

"I'll make it so you'll never want to go back to that business of yours ever again."

I was failing at my own dream of business ownership, but I wasn't sure I wanted to be back in the grind of a full time obligation. I told him I'd have to think about it since our meeting was not intended to discuss employment.

Instead of focusing on my business, I was enticed to work for him as the director of a failing senior citizen health care program. Although servicing senior citizens had always felt good, I wanted a challenge. Long-term care had become second nature to me and I could do it with my eyes closed if needed. If anything, I was looking for CEO opportunities or other consultant work, but definitely not another director's position.

After thinking about it and discussing it with Dalton and my parents, when Gabriel called, I accepted his offer and named my price. I didn't want to take the job, but I couldn't turn down that money! It was too good. I compromised myself again. I was doing something I knew I didn't want to do and wasn't right for me. My gut instinct told me not to do it, but to please others and boost up my bank account I put myself aside. I sold my soul to the devil.

Chapter 25

I quickly learned to appreciate the scripture that warns, *the love of money is the root of all evil*, because I had taken this job primarily for the money, and I was suffering the consequences. Although restructuring existing organizations was my forte, I found myself in a ritualistic pattern, and I despised the routine. This job was proving to be draining, mentally exhausting, and the commute was longer than I had anticipated. I was facing issues I had never faced before in my life. Racism, disrespect, lack of professionalism, sabotage and mind games were rampant. The administrator ruled as if he was in a third world country, as a cruel dictator where employee rights were non-existent. Never having experienced such an environment, I had extreme difficulty finding my niche.

I had always been a strong, respectful and kind professional. My hands were tied up in red tape, egos, and a fight for power between the administrator and the CEO. I had become the administrator's target, considering I was the only person in the entire facility who did not bow down to him and his demeaning ways. I had become an unforeseen challenge to the leaders in the facility while I walked and talked in my integrity. Every day, there were attempts to break me down emotionally and mentally as my limits were tested. Although I made great strides in revamping the department by restructuring every component and recouping a significant amount of finances, I felt out of place. I literally felt sick at the thought of going to work.

Each morning when I approached the parking lot, a heaviness descended on my chest and remained there until the moment I left at the end of the day. I had never felt such a weight in my life, even in my marriage. When I attempted to make a positive change, Gabriel, my so-called friend, would tell me to hold off, seeing that the administrator needed to review my recommendation. I knew more about my job and overall facility operations than he could ever know, and this was not what I had signed up for. Gabriel was flipping the script on me, because he originally said I was to deal directly with him and not the administrator. But the administrator had become more and more involved in my work.

I was working in Satan's Den! That's the only way I could describe it. The environment was indicative of what you would experience in hell. A life of torment, confusion, deception, lies, anguish, pain and fear. The entire staff operated in fear, and a feeling of anxiety was present throughout the facility. You could feel it in the halls and in the downtrodden spirits of the employees. Along with many others, I was suffocating. It was never meant for me to be here in the first place. I had resisted for good reasons, which I should have valued, but money had convinced me to come on board the ship, not knowing the destination was purgatory. My inner being was not at peace, and I needed to get out.

Sometimes on my ride home, I would call my parents and tell them of the torment I had endured. I thought they might be sympathetic and encourage me to leave so I could be happy.

"But the money is so good," they would say. "Block it out

and do your job. Don't cut your nose off to spite your face. Hold on until next year or until you find another job."

But I can't hold on. I'm dying inside. This place is hell and I can't survive working here for one more second. Despite this conviction, my mind betrayed me. *Your family could use that money. We can pay off some bills. Don't leave. It's not that bad. Twiddle your thumbs and get that money.* No one was hearing me, not even myself.

I stuck it out for the sake of others, like I always did. It didn't matter that another piece of me would die each time I was at work in Satan's Den. My well-being didn't matter because the money was more important to my family than my happiness. I was no longer self-assured since I allowed the dysfunction to mold me into someone else. Act like it's not happening. That's how you deal with it. Ignore anything that makes you uncomfortable. Do it, whether you like it or not. People are counting on you. Your feelings don't really matter because there is a financial benefit to your misery.

The darkness of that demonic job was so familiar to me that I attempted to fight my way through, like I had in other aspects of my life. The majority of my sixteen and a half year marriage was born and bred in obscurity. Although the fight had been hard, I knew I could make it through. I was tough and strong! So I thought. The weight of the job and my dysfunctional personal life had finally taken its toll. I wanted out. Out of everything. My job and my marriage had become too much to bear. I was lost and had no compass to find my way out of the wilderness. There was no direction, no map, no strategy or plan I could think of to get me out of the dead end street and on the right path.

Something had to give, and it was my marriage. The weight of holding everyone and everything up had finally beaten me down. I wasn't Superwoman, and there were no mortal powers left in me to juggle it all. I was failing in my life, unhappy in my marriage, and unsupported by the people I had loved, protected and sustained. Life had become unbearable as I struggled to figure out everything.

One day during a drive to Lincoln Park for a family outing, I decided it was time to end my marriage. As we approached a traffic light, Dalton was lecturing the kids about having to be the source of everyone's entertainment. "Take the lead sometimes yourselves!" he yelled.

Take the lead? When did you ever take the lead in anything? Instead of chastising the kids, he needed to convince himself of the "take the lead" bull he was dishing out. He continued his lecture for most of the ride to the park. At that point, no one was interested in going to the park anymore. *I need to save myself and my kids from this torture.* This life was not about living the way life was supposed to be. It was time to move on and get out of the suffocating death bag my kids and I had endured for too long.

We parked and the kids quickly jumped out. Dalton and I slowly exited the truck, each carrying our own heaviness. I remained silent as the kids walked a few feet ahead, occasionally looking back to see what Dalton and I were doing. Dalton was overwhelming me with a thousand questions, attempting to goad me. As with every argument we had, he asked, "Do you want to stay married?"

"No. No, I do not," I finally replied, and with that answer I felt free. He had asked me that question for nearly sixteen years, and my answer had always been the same until this day.

Surprised, he asked me again, almost as if he wasn't sure he had heard me correctly.

"No. I do not want to stay married anymore. I want out of this." I became more confident with each follow up question he asked.

"Are you sure?"

"Yes!" I said, looking him directly in his eyes. He quietly walked off and I caught up with the kids. Carter went to play pick-up basketball while Alisa obsessed about where Dalton was.

"Where's Daddy?" she asked.

"He's fine," I said, but she was not convinced.

Alisa spotted Dalton walking and ran over to him. She quickly returned and told me, "Daddy ignored me." Alisa and I watched Dalton pace back and forth, and then he walked out of our sight. "Is he leaving us?"

"No. He's fine," I said. I called Dalton on his cell phone to see if he was going to abandon us in the park or give us a ride back home. "Are you in the park?" I asked.

"Yeah," he said.

"Ok," I said, and hung up. The ride home was silent, but I was finally at peace.

Chapter 26

Dalton had gone through the stages of grief since our "walk in the park" turned tragic for him. Life for the kids and me continued as usual, and I spent my time planning my exit strategy. As much as I hated my job, I needed to stay put and save money for my future. I put my personal feelings aside and did what any mother would do to prepare for single parenthood.

The following weekend, Dalton and the kids went to Philadelphia to visit family, and I used the time alone to reflect. I called my friend, Emily, and discussed what was happening. I finally admitted to her that Dalton was not enough for me. It felt weird to say it out loud. Dalton had always felt he was not enough, and I spent so much time convincing him otherwise. But for the first time I could admit to myself. The Dalton he had become and the Anni I was now no longer fit.

From the time we met, Dalton had always carried a heaviness around him. He had a very complex backstory that encompassed a tangled adoption after he was surrendered by his birth mother. His adoptive family never seemed totally committed to his emotional care. Even after finding his birth mother and father years later, he still felt a void in his life and disconnected from both families. Due to the emotional turmoil of his past, after we got married Dalton had issues that I was forced to deal with.

As I described earlier, I had become the mother Dalton never had but desperately needed. I supported, nurtured, comforted and protected Dalton the way a mother would care for her children. However, he was a grown man. He was my husband. He needed me to love him unconditionally, like a mother, but I needed him to love me as a wife. I needed the love and support of a husband, but due to the tangled change of roles, I ended up loving Dalton in the way I loved my two children. I assumed the dysfunctional role because I thought there was no other option. Between the job from hell and Dalton, I was dead inside. I had to cut them both loose.

Dalton and the kids returned from their weekend in Philadelphia and I could see how lost he was. I still had love for him, but as a mother rather than a wife. It pained me to see "my son" suffering, but I had to stand my ground on the decision to dissolve our marriage. One morning after the kids had gone to school, Dalton began questioning me again and pleading with me not to leave. To avoid getting involved in the back and forth routine of another argument, I told Dalton that my decision was final. It wasn't open for discussion because I was not going to change my mind like I had in the past.

As I got ready to travel to work, Dalton asked me again to reconsider leaving him. He promised to do better, but he had no idea what the problem was, nor did he possess the tools to fix it. To help him understand I grabbed a plastic shopping bag, filled it with air and twisted the neck closed.

"This has been our life for the past sixteen and a half years. We got married in this bag and had two children in this bag. We have existed inside this empty asphyxiating world for way too long," I said. Looking confused, Dalton sat quietly. "Our entire married life has been inside this bag, with no air coming in or going out. Life cannot exist inside of a bag. Suffocation happens. Nothing can grow because there is no light, and we are dying a slow death inside this bag. The elements we need to survive and thrive as a family can never exist inside this bag. This bag is you! All the heaviness and betrayal you have unconsciously dragged into this marriage is inside this bag."

    I finally had Dalton's full attention. I let the air out of the bag and said, "I'm releasing myself and the kids from this bag." I balled the bag up in my hand, lifted the kitchen garbage can lid, tossed in the crumpled bag and slammed down the lid. "That's you in your death bag. We'll mourn for you, but like all deaths, with each passing day we'll learn to live without you. I will not and cannot allow myself or these kids to live in a death bag. We have to experience life and growth, and that bag represents neither."

    Dalton looked at me in amazement. "I don't want to die! I don't want to die!" he repeated. Dalton balled up his fist and pounded on the granite counter tops, repeatedly screaming out in pain. "Aaugh!" he yelled as the pain escaped his soul and filled the air. Dalton dropped to his knees and yelled, "God, help me! God, please help me!" His voice seemed to shake the foundation of the house.

    I stood nearby without touching him or attempting to console him. He needed to feel the pain, which had been buried so deep within him that he was oblivious to its existence. The pain that had ruled his whole life was bubbling to the surface. Dalton had done everything in his being to conceal his agony for fear of the destruction it would cause if he ever allowed it to come out. He had no control. The hurt he carried was being forced out by an unseen power. Dalton lay helpless on the kitchen floor in a fetal position, surrendering to the process of exorcising his demons. I cautiously remained distant as I witnessed "my son" being picked up and placed in the wilderness, with the possibility that he could find his way out. Although it was difficult to watch, I was not afraid.

Dalton slowly got up off the floor and headed to the kitchen sink. He pulled the removable nozzle from the faucet, turned on the cold water, and let the flow rain down upon his bald head, and down his neck and back. He exhaled loudly as he seemed to be cleansing himself of the dirt and grime he had cocooned himself with his whole life. I got a towel and handed it to him. Standing by the sink, he faced the wall and cradled his face inside the soft towel. When Dalton turned around, he was a weakened soul. A lost little boy. My heart wept for his anguish, but I refused to continue the role of mother. Therefore, I simply asked, "Are you ok?"

In a hoarse and trembling voice, Dalton said, "Thank you. Thank you."

"You're welcome," I replied. "I take it you're not going to work."

"No. No, I'm not. Can you call out for me?" he asked.

"No. You have to call yourself. You're capable," I said. He struggled to pick up the phone, but he made the call. In a deep, exhausted voice, he managed to do it without me.

"Are you going to be ok?" I asked.

"Yes. I'll rest today," he said. I grabbed my things and headed off to work. It was time for Dalton to grow up and emerge from the darkness a grown man.

Chapter 27

Dalton finally understood me, but it was not an easy road for him to travel. He struggled with letting me go and fighting to save himself. Finding his way out of the wilderness alone was a daunting task. I watched the turmoil within him take shape and prayed for him to come to terms with his demons. Despite my sympathy for Dalton, I continued to work on my exit plan. I was not going to let guilt convince me to go backward and live in that bag any longer. Usually I would feel sorry for him and go back to the lifeless ways of our existence, but this time was different. I was ready to live. Ready to grow. Ready to be free from all the "stuff" that had entrapped me for many years.

An important lesson I've learned along my journey is that as we move into adulthood, self-discovery is crucial to learn to be happy within ourselves. By the time we're ready to get married, we should know ourselves inside out and be confident about the decisions we make. Unfortunately, many couples get married because their biological clocks are ticking or they fall victim to the fantasy of living happily ever after. In my situation, I felt like I had no other choice but to go ahead with the wedding despite the red flags. I should have had the courage to follow my gut feelings and wait. Marriage is hard work, and to have any hope of success it requires mature people, who are self-assured in knowing who they are and what they want out of life. If you get married before you are ready, regardless of the reason, you're doing yourself and your mate a huge disservice. Loving someone isn't enough. You have to know and love yourself first.

Prior to my marriage, I was a free, independent person. I never felt burdened despite my parents' shortcomings. I always managed my way around the thorns of life. But I wasn't strong enough in my convictions to delay our marriage, and soon Dalton's darkened world was hard to escape. I had learned to surrender to the pain and adopt it as my own. No more. I was ready to take my life and soar on the wings of eagles. It was time for us to get to know ourselves outside of our marriage. We had no true sense of who we were as individuals.

During our preparation to separate, Dalton and I were amicable as we tried to move forward and co-exist in the same home at the same time. I had decided to explore moving after June, giving the kids time to finish the school year in their current schools. One afternoon I was sharing my potential plans with Dalton, and he started looking around the living room, dining room and den. "This house is bare. Empty. There are no pictures on the walls. There is no evidence of life in here," he said shamefully. "If you stand at our front door and look inside, you'll see every wall lacking personality, culture, or a sense of family. When you walk through every room of our house, there is not one item that indicates who lives here or what our family represents. This is a shame. How could we live this way? There is no life here."

Our home represented the empty shell of our lives. Although we had tried to decorate here or remodel there, the home was never complete. We had a nice kitchen and new furniture, but like our existence, a few disseminated pieces never brought anything together collectively. Our home was empty like our lives. Things were scattered about in every facet of our home and in our world, with the exception of our daughter's room.

Alisa was determined to do things differently. Her room was full of life and light, and it reflected who she was as a person. She liked bright, authentic colors such as yellows, orange, greens and blues. She had inspirational phrases in frames hanging on the walls. She had signs of nature such as elephants, owls and plants in various corners. Out of all the rooms in our house, Alisa was the only one with life. Alisa was that flower, thriving despite the odds. Even though she was submerged in the toxic air surrounding her parents, little by little she grew and bloomed. As Alisa developed her own thoughts and values, she had struggles as some teenagers do, but her room was always a safe haven for her when she needed to escape.

Although my son's room was certainly not as pretty as Alisa's, he was doing fine. He lived his life by his own rules, and he wouldn't allow our heaviness to cling to him. His personality was big and stubborn, and he was clear about being his own person. He was funny and enjoyed life. To Carter, life was fun, easy, and unbothered.

Kids are so innocent, but it's the parents that can dampen the light children are born with. Just let them be. Allow them to explore and discover who they are. Most parents have good intentions, but if we bring drama and burdens into our homes, we are the problem. My children and their vibrant spirits remind me that I need to live my life colorfully and by my own rules, unbothered and unafraid.

I was invited to a girlfriend get-away in Turks and Caicos with Terri, Michelle and Lynette. I know. I still had unpleasant memories from Miraval, but I'd like to think that I'm big enough to forgive, even if I couldn't forget. Perhaps their invitation was an effort to apologize for their hurtful actions in Miraval. Who knows? They were the only people in my life I was able to travel with and get away. I was invited and agreed to go. I needed this respite, and it couldn't have come at a more perfect time. It was an opportunity to shed the skin of my past and rejuvenate my soul.

We were fast approaching our departure date, and Michelle dropped out. Lynette, a college friend of Terri's, booked her flight separately since she was the only one leaving from New Jersey. Being a gambler, Terri was holding off booking her flight with hope of landing a great deal. I grew nervous about waiting and ending up paying an astronomical price, so I called Terri to convince her to book her flight with me. She declined and urged me to go ahead and make my reservation with the promise that she would be on the same flight.

If this is a girlfriend trip, why not book the flights together? (Red flag, Anni, but you are once again choosing to ignore it.) Terri wanted to hold out for a cheaper fare, but I was uncomfortable with her decision. Was she actually going on the trip, or would she back out at the last minute? Although Lynette and I graduated from college together, I didn't know her well enough to be going on a trip with just her.

Dalton, my parents, and a few other friends thought it was strange and advised me to cancel the trip. Giving Terri the benefit of the doubt and hopeful she wouldn't cancel, I held on. The days grew closer, and Terri had yet to book her flight. At this point, I was uncertain what was happening. I sent her text messages numerous times to inquire if her flight had been booked with no response. I called the travel agent to inquire if Terri had cancelled her trip, but I was assured she had not.

Finally, Terri sent me a text saying Michelle was trying to rebook the trip, but it was sold out. Was that the reason for the delay in booking the flight? (Another red flag.) A week before the trip I texted Terri, and again she didn't respond. With concerns coming from Dalton and my father, I cancelled the trip, fearing something wasn't right. I finally acknowledged the red flags that had been popping up everywhere during the planning of the trip.

The next day, Terri texted me to say she booked her flight and would be on the same flight as me. I texted back to tell her I cancelled my trip because it no longer fit with where I was in my life, and she responded, "I'm sorry to hear that." That's it! There was no frantic phone call to say, "Girl, what's going on? What happened? Why are you not going?" You know, the kind of reaction you would get from a *real* friend. Later, I sent her a text saying that her lack of communication and her cold response spoke volumes about our friendship, and the only reply I received was, "What do you want me to say?" Our twenty-seven year friendship ended with that last message. She proved to me in that last text that she did not value our friendship. It should have been obvious to me long ago, but I chose to ignore the fact.

With a non-refundable trip to be rescheduled, and no friends and no husband I wanted to be with on a vacation, I decided to take my kids on their first Caribbean trip after the school year ended. Traveling alone with the kids, especially out of the country, was not something I was used to, but I needed to get accustomed to doing things alone. As I explored the options with the travel agent, Dalton asked to go along. We had already started the process of separating, and I didn't think it was a good idea to have him join us. I wanted to start experiencing life without him, since that was quickly becoming my reality.

Although Dalton admitted that he was still trying to figure out his life, he made it clear he wanted to fight to keep his family together. Dalton felt this trip was life or death, and believed if I had the courage to travel without him, there would be no hope for our marriage upon my return. He wanted the opportunity to prove his ability to be a great husband and father outside of "the bag." Dalton knew where I stood and there were no promises of reconciliation made on my behalf. I agreed to let him go since we had not yet shared with the kids that we intended to separate and they would find it strange if Dalton was absent.

I rebooked the trip for the end of June through July 4. I made it perfectly clear to Dalton that the decision to allow him to join the vacation did not mean we were staying married. Dalton usually has a hard time getting specific vacation time off, especially over a holiday, and he did something I never thought he would do. He pleaded with his employer to let him have the time off, and admitted to his supervisor that if he did not go on this trip, his marriage would be over.

Dalton was a very private person, and under normal circumstances, he would never let anyone in on his personal life. He started wearing his heart on his sleeve for everyone to see. There was no shame and no secrets anymore. His life was falling apart, and he didn't hide it. After he revealed the honest reason for his request, his vacation time was approved. Dalton would have to face his fear of flying, but he was determined to make this trip at all costs. Dalton looked at me and said, "If I can only make it to the water at Turks and Caicos, I know our lives will be better."

Chapter 28

I had mixed emotions about Dalton going with the kids and me on vacation, but since it was about three months away, I tried to put it in the back of my mind. I had a lot of pressure to reconcile my marriage, and I needed to get away and clear my head. I decided to visit my cousin, Pam, in Virginia, and stop by to see a new friend, Raya, who I had met at the *Oprah Live Your Life* Tour. She sat directly in front of Dalton and me, and we have been good friends ever since. I arranged to visit with Raya first, since she was on the way. This was the first time Raya and I had seen each other since the Oprah experience.

We met in a quaint coffee shop near her home in Maryland, and we talked about how life had evolved since we attended the tour. We shared where we were on our journeys and offered each other encouraging words and support. It felt good to have a friend who understood me and the struggles that came along with life's ups and downs and offered genuine concern. Raya talked a lot about God and her reliance on Him to see her through life's challenges.

I didn't fully understand the dependency she had on God.

I thought I'd established a good relationship with God at Miraval, but that quickly dissolved as I was caught up in the whirlwind of my life. I had done all right by myself without God playing a major role, or so I thought. Listening to Raya talk about God made me wonder why I never had that understanding of Him. My mother's twin sister, Ruth, was a devout Christian, and she was the only person (other than Raya) who talked about God with such joy. God was not completely foreign to me, but He wasn't a part of my everyday life.

As I traveled towards Virginia from my stop in Maryland, I couldn't help but dwell on Raya's success. Since the Oprah tour, she had written, completed and published her first book. It made me realize that, since the tour, I was no closer to where I desired to be, even though I was excited and had good intentions. Maybe she was more driven than I was. Maybe I needed to be more focused. Yeah, that was it! I needed to concentrate more to reach my goals.

As I sat in traffic, something deep down inside spoke to me. *There's more than being focused and task oriented.* I ignored the voice, and I turned up the radio to distract myself from the unbelievable amount of traffic. Although the drive should have only taken a little over an hour, it was nearly two and a half hours later when I reached Pam's house. I pulled up to her front yard, and I jumped out of my car and into hers. She had been waiting on me to run errands, and she was expected at a talent show for some of the residents at the group home she owned and operated.

Pam is my first cousin on my father's side. She has the entrepreneur gene as well, as her dad and my dad owned their own trucking business together. As a child, I was always close to Pam, and I looked up to her the same way a little sister admires a big sister. She and I, along with my brother and a few other cousins, used to ride motorcycles in North Carolina. Our grandparents owned a large amount of land, which allowed us to roam free. Pam was a country girl at heart, and

I was born and raised in New York. Although she and I grew apart as we got older, we had recently started to communicate more often and made an effort to be a part of each other's adult lives.

Pam had the success I was endeavoring to achieve. She had done really well for herself, and my father would remind me that I could have had the same success if I had joined the Army like Pam did. The army life wasn't for me. I joined ROTC in college, albeit unwillingly, and I quickly confirmed that I was not cut out for that life after hearing I was going to be sleeping in a tent when the cadets went on a retreat to Fort Dix. The "Yes, Sir" and "No, Sir" didn't come natural for me, although I had southern roots. I was a true defiant New Yorker. Strong willed and independent. I was respectful, but I knew I wasn't cut out for the military.

After a late dinner, Pam and I finally found ourselves back at her house around midnight. It had been a long day, and I was ready for bed. Pam showed me around the guest room, and I quickly realized there was no TV. *This is going to be a long night,* I thought to myself. After I showered and got into bed, I laid my head on the pillow, and I couldn't help but think about my visit with Raya. For some reason, God was at the forefront of my mind, but I'd had a full day and I soon drifted off to sleep.

I quickly was reminded I don't sleep well without Dalton's presence. It seemed like I was up every thirty minutes, with random thoughts racing in and out of my mind. I finally dozed off and woke up around 6:30 am. I washed up, got dressed and sat in the kitchen until Pam joined me. Once she was up, we were off and running. We hit Starbucks for a morning pick me up and ran errands to buy supplies for the second group home she planned to open in less than a year.

What was I doing differently than Pam and Raya? They were making serious moves while I sat stagnant, watching life pass me by. Initially Pam knew very little about group homes, but she put in a significant amount of work to learn the details of operating a home and had done extensive research on the industry in general. I had years of experience with group homes, but when I visited Pam's facility, I quickly learned how she is raising the bar within the industry. Her homes are family centered, and it was obvious that love and care go into every detail. The fact that Pam, the owner, was front and center in the day-to-day operations was astounding.

This trip was providing me with more inspiration and motivation than I could have ever imagined. Everything that goes into being an entrepreneur is not all glitz and glam, and it requires planning, hard work and dedication. I needed to get it together, kick it up a notch or two, or three, and get myself moving. If Raya and Pam could do it, so could I.

Pam invited me to church on Sunday, but I told her I wanted to leave early and avoid the afternoon traffic. As I was getting my things ready to leave, I changed my mind and decided to go to church with her. Pam's congregation was unlike any church I had ever attended. The strict order that exists in most traditional churches was not present, and it had a casual, laid back, come-as-you-are atmosphere. There were no rules about what to wear, and people were dressed in shorts, sneakers, sweats, or whatever else they felt comfortable wearing. In the vestibule there was a table set up with coffee, sugar, a variety of creamers, an assortment of danishes, donuts, and muffins that parishioners could enjoy prior to entering the sanctuary.

Pam was obviously well known, and she stopped to talk with just about everyone we encountered. We took our seats in the front, and I looked around and saw how at ease everyone appeared. There was no pressure to be anything other than what we were. There was none of the rigid formality that is often seen in church. I thought about how my kids would love this church since they wouldn't have to get dressed up. I was in jeans, a tee shirt and sandals!

The theme of the sermon was *Cleaning Out Your Life*. The pastor talked about God and how the Holy Spirit empowers us by dwelling within us. God created each person with a purpose, and the Holy Spirit has the job to assist us in accomplishing our God given purpose. The preacher explained how the Spirit of God wants to breathe life into us, but the only way that can be done is if we surrender, because God will never force it on anyone.

Now, I had gone to church before, and I didn't recall anyone talking about discovering God's plan for ME or how to figure out MY purpose. This pastor focused on the scriptures from the book of Ezekiel about being in a valley with dry and broken bones, which we all seem to have visited at some point in our lives. God instructed Ezekiel to tell the bones, "I will put breath in you, and you will come to life." (Ezekiel 37:6 NIV.) God wants to breathe life into our bones, to restore us to the default mode He originally created.

In order to find victory, you must surrender. There is healing and help in a surrendered state. The earlier you submit, the shorter your journey in the valley. In this context, the valley was a place where old bones were stored. Bones you'd rather not deal with since they may have a significant amount of trauma, hurt and pain associated with them you'd rather soon forget. According to the pastor, the bones left behind cause us to live the stench of death in our life. However, the final verse of Ezekiel Chapter 37 provides God's unmistakable message. "I will put my Spirit in you and you will live." (Ezekiel 37:14 NIV.)

Chapter 29

My ride home was an interesting one. I kept the radio off for most of my six-hour ride and used the silence to absorb everything I had heard in church. The weekend had been about God and my acknowledgment of His absence in my life. I never knew how important God was in the life of a person. I had never given God serious thought until my ride home from Virginia and while on that tightrope at Miraval. Yes, I had been "saved" when I was a child. I professed my sins and accepted Jesus died on the cross, rose again, and that He is my Lord and Savior, but my knowledge about God was limited. My need for Him seemed to be much more prevalent now than in the past. I was going through a lot in my life, but I didn't feel like I could really share how I was feeling.

My parents were self-centered and speaking to them about anything happening in my life was a waste of time. It never did any good. Most people in my world were so self-absorbed that they rarely recognized when I needed help. I was always the go-to person when problems arose. If and when I decided to share an issue or concern, it was quickly brushed under the rug. "You'll be ok. You're smart, and you'll figure it out." I was the fixer, and no one ever saw me as the one who might need fixing. As I drove along I-95, I wondered who was going to help me since I was always the helper.

My getaway weekend, spending time with Pam and Raya, had been fantastic. It was nice to be around authentic woman who were supportive of my well-being and me personally. Their successes inspired me and I returned home with a renewed energy to face the challenges I had left behind. I had an optimistic attitude about my future. I went away to clear my head and I felt so much better. Even though I was anxious about Dalton going on vacation with the kids and me, I was looking forward to being away from Satan's Den for two weeks and basking in the beautiful Turks and Caicos.

This had been our dream vacation for a long time. It only took us six years and two sets of passports for the kids to get here since Alisa's and Carter's first set of passports had expired prior to ever receiving their first stamp. Nonetheless, we were ready to be on our way. This trip was going to be the kids' first overseas vacation, and they were fifteen and eleven years old at the time. We were all hopeful the journey would renew, restore and revive our lives! We each had great things to accomplish outside of that bag and I knew God (Yes, I was saying God) would realign our paths, our lives, and our dreams. I was praying (Yes, praying) and asking God for His wisdom, grace, and mercy to help us use this vacation to visualize the unseen, to hear His words of wisdom and feel His presence in all things. I was looking for another experience like my Swing and a Prayer challenge, where I would be able to leave my confusing thoughts, fears, doubts, and uncertainties behind. Although Dalton and I had different purposes for the trip, we both wanted to relax and let go of our worries over the next five days.

We flew my mother to New York for her to sit with our dog, as it was cheaper to fly her in than it was to board Kaiser in the kennel. She used our truck to drive us to the airport, where she dropped us off. We checked in with our luggage, got our tickets and easily made it through security, which can be the most stressful part of flying.

Dalton and the kids were excited, but I couldn't help thinking this was going to be our last family vacation. As I watched Dalton engage with the kids, I wondered if I was doing the right thing by deciding to dissolve the marriage. Dalton caught me deep in thought and asked, "What's wrong?"

"Nothing. Just thinking," I said.

"It's going to all work out. Believe me, it will come together. I have to get down to that water," he said confidently.

"All passengers seated in Rows 18 through 25 please come forward," the counter agent announced.

"That's us!" Dalton said with excitement. As we gathered our carry-on luggage and headed for the line, Dalton reached over and held my hand. "It's going to work out. Trust me." Dalton didn't even stress about flying, and he was usually so nervous he had to hit the bar prior to taking off. But he was different this time. As we boarded the plane, the kids and I sat on one side and Dalton had the aisle seat on the other side. Our flight was uneventful, and as we were coming in for a landing, the kids looked out the windows and were amazed at the beautiful colors of the water. They had never seen blue ocean water in their lives.

Upon our arrival Dalton took control of everything, which was a first because he usually stood back and let me handle things. On this trip, he emerged as a leader instead of a follower. He led us through customs with ease, found our transportation connection, loaded our luggage, and got us all seated in the van that we shared with other vacationers headed to the Beaches Resort. At the resort, we were greeted with rum punch, and the kids had a virgin version. We were seated in the lounge area waiting to check in when we heard there was a problem with our room. Who wants to hear that when they've just arrived? We booked through a travel agent to be assured everything would be perfect. I was not a happy camper.

Dalton said, "Anni, please, don't stress. I've got this. I'll handle everything." He met with the manager of the Beaches French Village and settled everything. She apologized and assured us she would do everything possible to make our stay perfect. We were escorted to our room, which was very nice. Instead of a king size bed, we had two queens and a trundle for the kids. "We want to eat, and head for the blue water!" the kids yelled in excitement.

"Ok. Let's do it!" Dalton said, equally excited. We hurried and changed into our swimsuits, and sat down at the first restaurant we came upon. It was an all-inclusive resort, and it felt strange getting up without paying the bill or leaving a tip on the table. We asked for directions to the beach and off we went. As we walked towards the beach, Carter saw the pool, ran, and jumped in. He laughed and splashed around for a few minutes, but Dalton was intent on getting to the beach.

We approached the beach and I noticed Dalton became quiet and focused as he stared at the gorgeous water of the Atlantic Ocean. I remembered the statement he had made when he asked if he could come on this trip with us. *If I can only make it to the water at Turks and Caicos, I know our lives will be better.* Did he think something magical was going to happen? I was quickly distracted by the beautiful surroundings and the plan to enjoy every moment of this get away.

We shed ourselves of our cover-ups and tee shirts, and the kids ran toward the water, smiling ear to ear. Alisa was normally afraid of getting her hair wet due to the massive amount of hair she has as she was extremely tender-headed. She bent over and cupped her hands together to gather some water, and then she dripped the water over her head. With that action, Alisa proved she wanted to be herself. She desired the freedom to be carefree and not worry about her hair or anything else. Carter ran into the waves, full speed ahead, splashing water around until he dove in, to resurface with his face to the sun.

Dalton approached the water with his eyes closed, as if he was praying before entering. He took one step, then two, then three, and as he continued, he slowly lifted his arms high above his head. With his fist clinched, he raised his face to the sky and entered the water. It was as if he was being baptized. He walked in, fist still held high, until the water was up to his chest and his arms straight up, as far as they would reach. He slowly went under the water, and the only thing visible was his raised fists. He emerged from the water and turned around to face me. With his arms fully extended, Dalton yelled at the top of his lungs, "I'm here! I'm here! We're here! I'm free."

Life as we knew it was about to change, and I felt it in that instant. "Come in!" my family shouted to me. I stayed a few more minutes to snap some pictures, and then I went to the water and walked in. Dalton came drifting over to me, saying, "I see you. I see you. I want you to know that I can see you." I had never been seen. No one saw who I was, or what I carried, or the sacrifices I had made. I looked into his eyes, and I felt seen for the first time in a long time.

The trip was like nothing we'd ever experienced. Our connection as a family was stronger than it had ever been. Everyone felt a sense of freedom, a rebirth, and I didn't have to worry about anything. There was no stress, no pressure, no negativity, and no bag. Just peace. We spent time exploring the resort with a lightness and sense of determination.

One night Dalton and I took a stroll and sat by the pool to reflect on the past few months. Dalton vowed to do better and be better. He asked for a fair chance at proving he could be all I ever wanted in a husband and friend. He begged me not to give up on our family and he promised to do whatever was required to regain my trust in him as a man, and not the little boy I had dealt with over the years. Although I knew he meant what he was saying, I believed actions spoke louder than words, and I made no promises. I had an inner desire to focus on my needs, my life plan, and myself before I could be content, and he needed to do the same. Then we could talk about staying together.

We talked openly and honestly about what we, as individuals, desired out of life because figuring out ourselves had to be the catalyst to drive everything else. If it was meant for us to remain together, we had to stay committed to working on ourselves first and foremost. We needed to find our friendship and reconnect to the things that brought us joy. We were both committed to re-establishing our friendship. We ended our vacation rejuvenated and excited about life. The kids made it clear that they were no longer interested in swimming in brown beach water. Every vacation from here on out must be where there was blue water.

Chapter 30

A few months after our vacation I started attending a Bible study group at church every Wednesday. Pam's pastor had piqued my interest in God, and I needed to spend some time getting to know more about the God Raya talked so highly of. The study themes varied week to week, but the focus of the series was why the church is important and what you believe matters. The studies met me exactly where I was, as a person new to the church. I knew nothing about church, the Bible, or the stories most religious folk talk about. I only knew one scripture, which I learned in a Sunday school class I attended while visiting my Aunt Ruth: "Faith is the substance of things hoped for, the evidence of things not seen." (Hebrews 11:1 KJV.) I could not tell you Bible stories, and I didn't know the purpose of Palm Sunday or Easter. I never learned why we celebrate the things we do and, as a forty-four year old woman, I should have been ashamed, but honestly I was not. I was happy to stand in my truth, and acknowledge what I knew or lacked.

The Bible study was perfect for me because it gave me a chance to learn without anyone judging me. During the sessions, Pastor Livingston broke down the Bible, explained the lessons it taught and the purpose of the church in language that was easy to understand. This was pre-school for me, and maybe it would help me deal with the lack of direction I seemed to possess. This was right on time!

I was so thankful that Raya's influence led me to get involved in the Bible study more diligently. One day Raya called me to see how I was doing. It had been a difficult day, and I had spent most of the morning crying and feeling depressed. I told her I was completely lost in my attempts to get my business off the ground. All my efforts over the past four years had fallen flat, and I didn't know what I was doing wrong or how to fix it.

Raya suggested that I write out my life goals and the tasks that were needed to complete each one. Although she was speaking clearly, I was unable to comprehend what she was saying. My mind was in a total fog. There was something deeper going on. It was more profound than writing down goals and tasks. My life was a roller coaster. Going uphill with Bible study, Oprah, Turks and Caicos, and then drastic twists and freefalls with my business attempts, Dalton, my self-doubt, and Satan's Den. I didn't know when I was going to be up and when I was going to be down. It was as if I was standing on the outskirts and watching someone else's life. This life was not meant to be mine, and I knew it.

"I'm trapped and can't find my way out," I told Raya.

All these years I had thought the root of my problem was Dalton and the baggage he brought with him. Since our return from Turks and Caicos, he had been working on himself and vowed never to return to the death bag I had thrown in the garbage. It was me. I had my own baggage.

"Have church right now," Raya said. "Invite God into your heart. Anni, God is strongly moving you to a season of change that will fulfill you and lead you to His purpose. Believe in that."

Raya could sense that I was struggling with issues more

detailed than she felt comfortable addressing. She recommended that I speak to her life coach, who had helped her get unstuck. *I don't need a professional,* I thought. *Or do I?* Raya gave me Dr. Benton's number and insisted I call him as soon as possible. "Please, Anni. Call him," she said before hanging up. I stared at the number in disbelief, as I attempted to grasp that I needed professional help. *I am the professional.* I dialed the number and hung up before it connected. *I don't need any help. I can figure this out like I always do.* As I convinced myself not to call, I started crying. *Something must really be wrong. Maybe I do need help. Call him,* my mind said. *Call him now!*

I picked up the phone again and dialed the number. Good, I got his voicemail. "Hi, my name is Anni Johnson, and I was referred by Raya, who suggested I call you. She believes you can help me with getting my business off the ground." I left my phone number and started writing an outline in preparation for the call back. My outline focused on who I was, my passions, talents, business purpose, challenges, what I've been through over the past few years in my marriage, and life goals.

Chapter 31

Dr. Benton called back the same day to schedule our initial session over the phone for 2:45 pm that afternoon. I had decided to drive to the park so I could have some quiet time before the session. My children got home from school around that same time and I needed some privacy so I could talk candidly with Dr. Benton. As 2:45 pm approached, I became anxious. I had been in marital therapy sessions, but this felt different. My back was up against the wall because this was all about me, and there were so many aspects of my life that I had been unable to conquer. I needed help, but I was reluctant whereas accepting help meant I had failed in my ability to solve my own problems. I wasn't sure I was ready to accept that.

Dr. Benton called exactly at 2:45 pm. There was no small talk and he started asking questions to ascertain why I was calling him. "Top five things about you," he asked. Wow, I couldn't believe I stumbled to explain who I was using five words.

"Determined, compassionate, family oriented, loyal, and a great mom," was my answer.

"What do you see as your weakness?" he asked.

"Being vulnerable," I said without hesitation. I tried to paint the perfect picture of my life by sharing that I had a husband, two healthy kids, a dog, a great job and was living the American dream, but Dr. Benton saw past all the bull I was shoveling. He asked about the health of my marriage, and I was completely honest about the problems Dalton and I had from day one. I told him how I had to be the mastermind in our marriage by taking control of everything. I explained that because Dalton was rarely emotionally capable, he had not been an effective leader of our family.

"Tell me about your father," Dr. Benton said. I described my father as selfish. He had lived a double life ever since I was born, and probably even before that. My father loved me, and he would do anything for me. I was his favorite and he wasn't shy to show it. I knew it wasn't right for him to favor me over my brother. I had always viewed my father as a habitual liar. I felt he was never invested in our family, and we were not a priority in his life.

Dr. Benton explained how important a father's role is in developing their daughters. A father who is in tune with God gives his daughter confidence. A father molds, guides, and sets standards for a young girl, so she'll become a functioning, well-balanced adult. A father showers his daughter with verbal affirmations, which are crucial for a young girl's development and self-esteem. A father shows a girl how to choose a husband, based on his actions and treatment of the child's mother.

As Dr. Benton continued to talk about all the things a father should do, I was brought back to my childhood, which had been infused with betrayal, lies, deceit and pain. It was my responsibility to keep the family together. I was the glue to my parents' marriage. I was the bridge between my brother, Owen, and my parents. I was the referee during the verbal fights. I was the core of the family, and the family's survival depended on me, just like in my marriage.

I learned not to be dependent on any man for anything. I wore the pants in my life. That was a lot of weight for a young girl to bear. My father was physically present, but not involved in our lives. My mother had so much on her plate coping with my father's infidelity that she did the best she knew how. She didn't have the capacity to give us anything emotionally because her spirit had been used up, and she lived in survival mode. I know my mother loved us, and she made sacrifices to make sure my brother and I didn't want for anything. Nevertheless, there was a price to be paid for a mother who wasn't emotionally available. Even if she wanted to be, she couldn't.

The more I shared about my marriage, the more Dr. Benton pointed out some similarities between Dalton and my father. I had never imagined Dalton being like my father. They seemed like total opposites to me, but it wasn't the obvious that made them similar. My mother took control of the home because, although my father was present, he was emotionally and mentally absent, exactly like Dalton. My dad worked at night, and Dalton picked up another job and he was barely at home. My dad was unfaithful and so was Dalton, but honestly, my dad had Dalton beat on this issue. My mom wore the pants, and so did I. My mom did not have a husband to take care of her, and neither did I.

"You have to let your husband take care of you," Dr. Benton said.

"Ha!" I said with a laugh. "I have been taking care of Dalton our entire marriage. He wouldn't know the first thing to do for me."

"You have to let go and give people a chance to carry you and your burdens," Dr. Benton said.

"Who's going to do that?" I asked.

"Your husband," he said confidently. Dr. Benton explained the need for Dalton to take care of me. On this journey, I had to give up everything I thought was true but in fact was not. I had to allow Dalton to support me in ways he had never done before, not even for himself. Dalton was going to be forced to learn how to take care of a wife he barely understood. My behavior from the very beginning had made it clear that I didn't need him. Toilet clogged - I can fix it. Picture needs hanging - I can do it. Roof needs repair - I'll see that it gets done. Car needs service - I'll take care of that too. Kids have conflict at school - I'm on it! I did everything.

Dr. Benton made it clear that the first step on this journey was to allow myself to be 100 per cent cared for by Dalton. That meant, letting him take control over everything in our home, for our children, and anything that required leadership. Dalton was to do it, and do it solely by himself. He was to assume all the responsibilities that had been established early in our relationship as my role. My responsibility was to embrace not doing anything I didn't want to do. It was as if I was being asked to be an infant all over again.

As we continued, Dr. Benton talked about toxic relationships and how they must be removed from our lives. Toxic people are like infections or a growth that gets bigger and nastier over time. Without surgery or antibiotics, they have a tendency to spread and affect other parts of the body. You can never be healthy if you refuse to treat the disease. "If you don't cut them off at the source, they'll keep going until they destroy you," he said. "Your parents are toxic. You have to cut them off. You have to essentially divorce them."

"Say what!" I exclaimed. I was blown away by this concept. My parents are a part of my life. Yes, we have a strained relationship at times, but separating from them was not an option. Dr. Benton tried to convince me that keeping my parents involved in my day-to-day life was going to be counterproductive. I needed to remove them from my life as I tried to sort out the details of why I felt stuck. He believed they were a part of the big picture, and why I was unable to move forward and live the life I so desired. Give up on my parents?

Is this man crazy? Dr. Benton reiterated the need for space and separation from anything or anyone that was toxic, even if it was my parents.

In addition to his other suggestions, Dr. Benton wanted me to incorporate what he called, "couch ministry." Couch ministry is pretty much sitting in a comfortable place in your home where you can have quiet time, pray, read, talk to God, and eventually address the issues that have a hold on your life. It sounded crazy to me to give up my job, put all the responsibilities on a man that has never had them before, separate from my "toxic" parents and sit on the couch in my living room every single day.

"Are you sure you want to travel down this road?" Dr. Benton asked. "This journey will be hard, and you have to be prepared to face some difficult challenges along the way." Dr. Benton summarized his recommendations, which were:

#1 Divorce my parents. There was to be no contact at all, which also included my children being separated from their grandparents. No phone calls, no visits, no text or emails.

#2 Quit my job. It was a toxic environment and had to be eliminated to find the space for healing.

#3 Let my husband take care of me by assuming the role of leader in the family.

Dr. Benton emphasized that I had to accept and embrace the "selfish season" I required in order to heal. He said I needed to stop caring for everyone and allow them to care for me. Who are "them?" My parents? My husband? My kids? Friends? I think not! Dr. Benton believed the people I've cared for all these years are going to step right up and start taking care of me? That's a laugh! No one has ever cared for me, except me.

"It's time for you to sit in vulnerability with God and unblock the hold that has been placed on your life," Dr. Benton said. A hold on my life? Did he not hear me explain how successful I was because of my hard work, my will, and my drive? What does "sit in vulnerability with God" even mean? "God has got to pull you out of the pit you have been living in," Dr. Benton explained. "The pit where all of your brokenness exists. The pit where your pain and suffering is. The pit where your fears have been dwelling."

I remembered the sermon at Cousin Pam's church, when the pastor talked about the dried up bones on the floor of the valley. The things you want forgotten and have buried, never to dig up again. The unresolved issues, swept under the rug to avoid facing the emotional pain those issues may have caused. The pit is where the bones of your life reside, dormant. Waiting for you to hit a brick wall, or suffer some loss, betrayal, trial or obstacle you can't seem to climb over. The pit is where the beginning of the life you want resides. At the end of the story about the bones, God says, "I am going to open your graves and bring you up from them." (Ezekiel 37:12 NIV.)

"Do you have the courage, the strength, and the will to go there? To sit in vulnerability so God can pull you out of the pit?" Dr. Benton asked. "If you want to change, it's time to initiate your couch ministry and establish your relationship with God so you can get unstuck. You have to take this time and reflect on why you are where you are in life."

Was I ready to face a God I had never really known in the first place? What was God actually going to do that I hadn't already done? I didn't even know what it meant to get in a relationship with God. Who has time to sit on a couch all day anyway?

We ended our conversation, and I still didn't know what to do. I was feeling like talking to Dr. Benton was a waste of time and money. It seemed this guy couldn't even help me with what I really needed, which was getting my business off the ground. All I wanted was a little motivation and a nudge in the right direction, and I knew it will take off. He was trying to make it personal. I didn't need these sessions, especially with someone who was talking recklessly about divorcing my parents and leaving my lucrative paying job.

Chapter 32

As I drove home from the park after talking to Dr. Benton, I felt misunderstood. My expectations were completely different from what I had received. Some of the points resonated with me, but most didn't. I was frustrated. It seemed that the good doctor had overlooked why I had called him, which was to help me get unstuck and launch my business. Tears began to roll down my cheeks, and I drove home in silence, trying to absorb everything and imagine a life without my parents if I chose to heed Dr. Benton's advice. It felt like I was already mourning their loss.

After arriving home and pulling into the driveway, I sat in the car for a few minutes. I called Dalton and shared the highlights of my session. He was silent. I told him that it had been recommended that he assume all the responsibility and leadership of the family, while I curl up in a ball on the couch every day. I think the shock of this was too much, because all Dalton could say was, "That's crazy. That's completely crazy."

Neither one of us knew exactly how to process this information or envision what implementing the suggestions would look like realistically. We both concluded that divorcing my parents was out of the question. Dalton admitted that he would be willing to take care of me and be a leader for our family, but I had to accept his way of doing things without interjecting. Now, that was going to be the real challenge! Me keeping my mouth shut while Dalton attempted to navigate the intricate details of my world and everything I juggled 24/7. We were willing to explore this journey, with the goal of figuring out how to get my business off the ground. If this was where I needed to start, so be it. *How hard could this really be?* I thought.

I began by looking over my childhood photos, hoping to see something meaningful or tap into a memory. Some thought that would evoke emotions, similar to the ones that came over me the day Tyrese's song played on the radio while I was stuck in traffic. The photo albums were huge and stuffed with photos falling out of the three-ring binder struggling to keep the forty-year-old book together. Small 3x5 pictures and Polaroids had faded dates written on them, and the clear plastic that was meant to keep the photos in place had lost its adhesiveness. The see-through film that originally served its purpose was now wrinkled, cracked and useless.

Despite the poor condition of the photo albums, I perused the pictures and delighted in the memories. I was flooded with tears as I witnessed the bond between brother and sister, annual Father's Day barbeques, and pictures of our countless trips to North Carolina. I was happy in those photos and deeply loved by my family. My father worked nights and, looking back, I would say my mom functioned much like a single mother. When my father wasn't working, he was either asleep or hanging out somewhere else.

There were pictures of me, my mother and Owen enjoying our annual trips to Pinegrove Dude Ranch with my mother's close friends. We would go horseback riding, snow and grass skiing (grass skiing was the best!), swimming, and having a fun time. My mother was (and still is) a fun person. She made sure we had the best of the best - the newest toys, fly clothes, the latest sneakers, leather bomber jackets, and anything else we wanted. Although she carried a lot of burdens, she tried to give her children the finest of what she had to offer.

Owen and I grew up in Queens, New York, and there were countless photos of us taken during that time. Pictures of iron skates (with the key), skateboards, tag, bike riding, sledding, baseball, hopscotch, and skelly (which was painted onto our driveway) filled the pages of our family albums. Looking through the photo albums actually lifted my spirits. It made me feel good about where I came from and reminded me about the love of my family. Although shy, I was a strong-minded kid. I always stood up for what was right and would never tolerate anything that did not fall in line with my standards. Yes, even as a small child I was tenacious.

My brother didn't always get a fair deal from our father, so I felt compelled to stand up for Owen and shield him against my father. I became the go-to person for my mother and my brother when my father did things wrong or was out of line. I was my mother's emotional protector, my brother's keeper and advocate, my father's buffer, the leader of the house, and maintained the role of "the responsible one." I had supported my family emotionally for most of my forty-four years. I did everything possible to make life manageable for us while being a perfect daughter and sister. So, why was my life not perfect?

Chapter 33

I decided to take a chance on this therapy thing and see where it went. Dr. Benton said I wouldn't be able to get unstuck until I had time to heal. Although I wasn't sure exactly what I was healing *from*, I was a bit curious to see where it would lead. Maybe I could get something out of it that would eventually help my business. As a bonus, I might be able to address the overwhelming feelings I had in managing a family and working full time. Perhaps dealing with these issues would overlap and help my marriage too.

    I set up a weekly schedule where I chatted with Dr. Benton via phone every Monday at 1:00 pm. With each session, the theme of divorcing my parents became much more prevalent. I continued to talk to them every day, like I always did, but for some reason the conversations were becoming difficult. I shared a lot of my day with my parents – what the kids were up to, any problems I was having, my stress at work, as well as dumb things Dalton would say or do. Since Dr. Benton had planted a seed of doubt, I began to notice that when I shared details of my life with my parents the conversation became stressful. I was overwhelmed, and it felt like I was drowning. The therapy sessions created a new awareness of the toxicity around me. I was living in a constant state of panic as I attempted to juggle working, my responsibilities and the recommendations Dr. Benton was suggesting.

Dalton tried to take the lead, but my control wouldn't let him, so most of the time he would back off. I was finding it hard to catch my breath. In an effort to help my parents understand me, I tried to discuss the issues with them. After sharing my challenges, they would sing over the phone, "You can do it. You're smart. I wouldn't leave that job because you're making a lot of money. The kids need you to do x, y, and z for them." What I heard from them and everyone around me was, "I'm hungry. I need. I want." The demands on me had gotten to be too much. Was I going crazy? I could barely hear myself think.

My parents were sucking the life out of me. They were constantly complaining about each other and putting me in the middle of all the drama I had secretly held together and kept from the world's view. My brother's death was expanding within my neck and pressing against my throat, nearly suffocating me. My daughter was struggling to deal with several teenage issues, including a lack of authentic friends, standing firm in her beliefs and not caving in to peer pressure, but her decision to withdraw from life was happening right before my eyes and I couldn't help her. The betrayal of my husband oozed out of the open wounds that covered my body and infected the core of my being. His brief attempts to take care of me only served to confirm that I did a much better job than he could ever do.

Once again, I was face to face with the brick wall. I believed it existed due to my inability to get my business off the ground. I was beginning to recognize that the wall represented something much deeper than my business. I was unraveling. I could no longer hide the imperfections that took up residence in the deepest part of my core. I was the sacrificial goat that had been slaughtered to protect my family from their own destructive ways. I realized I had always been invisible to the ones who said they loved me. My needs, my cares, my wants were never acknowledged. Everyone was selfish. Despite her efforts to be generous and loving toward me and my brother, even my mother failed me because she was emotionally absent. There was no one to care for me, the invisible woman. Why would I entrust my life to people who refused to see me?

I'd become numb to my painful experiences. I seem to have learned to alienate myself from any emotions and ignore what was wrong. I watched my mother brush off my father's infidelity with several other women, and that he had fathered four children with another woman while still married to my mom. She had been totally overwhelmed, working full time and caring for me and my brother in addition to countless extended family members. A child is impressionable and absorbs the characteristics of what's being played out in their home. Although I was only a child, it was understood that any problem, no matter how big or small, was my responsibility.

I always had to be in control of my emotions since showing any would send my mother into a tailspin. She had her own problems to deal with, and the last thing she needed was to deal with someone else's emotions. I was responsible for many things, primarily keeping my brother's wild side under wraps so my father wouldn't penalize Owen for his frustration of being trapped in a family he never wanted. I had to keep everyone in check. This was a tall order for a small kid. I learned from my mother, you suck it up no matter how painful, and you move through it.

After nearly a month of weekly therapy sessions and practicing my couch ministry off and on, I quit my job and divorced my parents. Quitting my job was easy because each day I spent at Satan's Den was slicing away another piece of my soul, and I had known from the beginning that it was the wrong decision. Separating from my parents was the hardest thing I ever had to do, and the pain of it was debilitating. It felt like a death had occurred. I spent most of my days crying and mourning their loss. I started sitting on the couch every morning, wondering why I allowed myself to go through this.

Weeks of the same routine went by, and one day I heard a whisper. *Come to me. Come to me.* I looked around, but I knew I was the only one in the house aside from Kaiser, and the dog wasn't talking. At that time, I was in total despair. My heart wept because the separation from my parents was excruciating. My life was in shambles. I was an unemployed college graduate who was sitting on her couch crying every day, and I had no idea what to do with my life anymore.

Thoughts ran through my mind. *Suck it up, you baby, and stop your crying.* Yeah, I told myself. *I'm not a crier. I'm a doer. Crying isn't going to get me anywhere.* I willed myself to get off the couch and try to focus on other things. *Stop distracting yourself and feel the pain,* the voice said. Was this my imagination or was God actually talking to me? I had heard stories of God talking to people, but come on! This couldn't be real. I was sure this was my mind playing tricks on me. I needed to get myself in gear and either get my business moving or find another job. I couldn't sit on the couch every day in silence.

You can't do it, the voice said. My mind was telling me I wasn't strong enough to endure the process, but my heart was saying to get back on the couch and push forward. I forced myself to sit there in silence day-in and day-out, waiting to see what would happen. One morning, I grabbed my Bible and landed on Isaiah 41:10 (NIV). "So do not fear, for I am with you; do not be dismayed, for I am your God. I will strengthen you and help you; I will uphold you with my righteous right hand." As I reflected on that passage, I decided to take the couch ministry seriously. I sat on the couch every morning. I started with prayer, read scripture and devotionals from Charles Stanley, and sat in silence for hours until my children returned home from school.

My morning routines stayed consistent. I got up, made

everyone breakfast, washed laundry, and made up all the beds. I sat on the couch, and sometimes thought how stupid I felt sitting there. I grabbed and read my *In Touch Ministry Daily Devotional* and referenced the scripture noted in the passage and read that as well. After that, I sat in silence and wondered what I was doing. I felt like a failure sitting on the couch waiting on God. It was a joke.

Chapter 34

One day as I meditated, the voice spoke to me. *It's time to go there.* Go where? I wondered. *Down there. The pit. Come with me. Let me show you something.* I closed my eyes and envisioned myself going down a flight of stairs. The place was dark, and the stairs were old and broken in several places. I groped to make my way down, and it was cold and scary. I wanted to open my eyes because the thought of what was lurking in the dark was too much to handle, but I didn't. I struggled with my footing on the uneven steps, and I seemed to be crushing whatever was under my feet.

Do you see them all scattered about? These are your bones.

"My bones?" I questioned.

Yes, the bones of resentment, hatred, unforgiveness, and everything else that has gone unresolved and swept under the rug in your life.

"I don't understand," I said.

The experiences you have had in your life that were never fully resolved are down here. You must acknowledge these bones one by one in order to move forward. If you do not, you will forever be stuck. I opened my eyes and found myself still sitting on the couch in my living room. Had I fallen asleep? Maybe I was dreaming.

Refusing to acknowledge the vision, I got off the couch and started preparing after school snacks for my kids.

The next morning, I followed the same routine. I read my daily devotional and Bible scripture, and sat in silence. This time I reflected on what had happened the day before, and a flood of emotions came over me. I started to cry uncontrollably. The anguish of being separated from my parents was getting to me. I screamed out to God, "Why is this happening?"

You have to acknowledge these hurts in order to move forward.

I didn't know what was going on, and I was hysterical. Kaiser approached me in an effort to console me and he nudged my leg, ultimately resting his face in my lap. I fell to the floor on my knees, with my face in my hands and screamed as I rocked back and forth. "Help me. Somebody help me!" I yelled. As I cried, I thought about my brother, my aunt and every one of the losses I had experienced. I wanted someone to console me and tell me it was ok, but there was no one there. I wept for what seemed like hours.

I'm here. I'm with you. You don't need anyone else. I am enough, and I am what you need.

"Who are you?" I asked.

"I'm God!"

I jumped up in fear. I was blinded by the blur of tears, and I wiped my eyes as I tried to gain my composure. I thought for sure I was going crazy. I wasn't dreaming because I was wide awake, standing in my living room with snot and tears running down my face. Physically, I was doing ok, but mentally I was going bat crazy. I felt embarrassed by my behavior on the floor, sobbing like a child, but part of me didn't care.

The more I sat on the couch and continued my weekly sessions with Dr. Benton, the more pain was revealed. Giving myself permission to allow my pain to come to the surface was a pivotal moment on my journey. Never acknowledging the grief I carried or understanding why I felt responsible for everyone and everything contributed to the situation where I found myself. It was only a matter of time before I had to face facts and deal with the burdens that had been cast on me. My mother shouldered burdens, and she passed that obligation on to me, as it was probably passed on by her mother. In hindsight, I could see that I was doing the same exact thing to my daughter by forcing her to be independent and in control, and never show emotion. "Be strong and deal with it," I told her constantly. "Don't be a baby. Stop your crying and whining. When I was your age, I did it all by myself." I was dumping on my daughter what had been dumped on to me.

Part of addressing the misery caused by others is to offer forgiveness. Forgiveness doesn't mean you forget, but it frees you of the responsibility and breaks the chain that tied you to it. Although forgiveness can open doors to reconciliation, it's often more beneficial for you than it is for the person you are forgiving. Unforgiveness destroys. It eats away at you piece by piece and over time, you can become infected with countless diseases as the poisonous effects of unforgiveness penetrate your body.

I have been tested for autoimmune disease numerous times because my body showed signs of it being present. I have multiple nodules on the upper and lower region of both of my lungs, and there is no known origin. My pituitary gland is malfunctioning, and despite countless exams and tests, there is no explanation as to why I no longer have my menstrual cycle. I have elevated ocular pressure in both eyes, and currently need eye drops for relief. Stress is a major factor in unresolved issues, along with high blood pressure and anxiety. Unforgiveness takes its toll mentally and physically.

Dr. Benton suggested I write a letter to my mother and father, documenting my complaints and my need to forgive them. This was the start of acknowledging how my parents made me feel when I was a child and even as an adult. I didn't think I had a lot to say to my parents. Even though we had our issues, I'd always viewed them as good people. However, as I sat down and truthfully thought about my life, I had plenty to say. With each thought, my childhood anguish bubbled to the surface. My father played a much bigger role in my distress than my mother due to the way he treated her and my brother. I began to cry like a baby, wanting to be held and comforted, as the flood of emotions poured through every crevasse of my being.

"I'm not forgiving you because..." is a message people often give to make it clear they want to continue holding someone responsible for their suffering. In fact, you cause yourself and others more harm by allowing past mistakes to fester and refusing to forgive.

As I began to think about what I wanted to say in the letters to my parents, I went back into my childhood so I wouldn't leave any stone unturned. I wanted to air out everything. Of course, I was concerned about hurting their feelings, but the agony of holding on had proven to be devastating. I had spent my whole life protecting my parents from my true feelings or anything that caused them discomfort, because they were always so caught up in their own worlds and I didn't want to complicate things. I'd always seen them as fragile, and it was my strength that kept them intact. In order for me to remove myself from underneath this black cloud, I was willing to give it a shot.

Chapter 35

*After weeks of going back and forth, I decided
to write down my points of forgiveness,
starting with my mother.*

Mom, I forgive you for not having the courage to leave your toxic marriage, for not seeing the value in yourself to know that you deserved better. Mom, I forgive you for believing we were better off staying with Dad even though he showed you who he was time and time again. I forgive you for exposing us to a home life that robbed us of the promise to live a healthy and happy childhood. I forgive you for being naive and trusting people when you shouldn't, especially the time when I was twelve years old and you left me to be examined by a male doctor, who insisted you leave the room. I begged you not to leave me alone but you did, and the doctor proved to be inappropriate in his examination of my private area. I felt abandoned by the person who was supposed to protect me. Due to this experience, I learned that I had to take care of myself and never allow myself to be vulnerable again. Mom, I forgive you for not knowing who I was as your daughter and ignoring me when I verbalized being uncomfortable with people and places. I forgive you for sending me to a three-week sleep away camp when I was eight years old, knowing I was a shy kid who didn't make friends easily. I was afraid and begged you not to send me away.

Mom, I forgive you for pushing me away when I had a dream that something bad had happened to you, and I awoke crying hysterically. I pleaded with you not to get on the train to go to work, but instead you shoved me aside and said, "Get off me. I don't have time for this. I have to go to work." I was left crying and spent the whole day wondering if you were ever going to make it back home. I learned that my feelings didn't matter. There was no use for me to display any emotions, because they were usually ignored. I forgive you for believing Owen and I would have been better off without you as you attempted to escape the pain that consumed you. You were all we had at that time, and I forgive you for not seeing your importance in our lives.

I forgive you for not being emotionally available to me, where I could feel safe telling you things a mother and daughter should share with one another. I forgive you for not nurturing me the way a mom nurtures a daughter – hugging me, telling me you love me, letting me cry on your shoulder when I needed it, and praising me when I did something good. I never received any genuine affection from either you or Dad, which has made it hard for me to be an affectionate wife and mother. I needed physical comfort and verbal affirmation to know I was good enough.

I forgive you for making me feel I had to be perfect. I forgive you for making simple mistakes feel like a death sentence. I forgive you for making me feel guilty when I needed to be selfish and take care of my own needs. I forgive you for not recognizing when I was falling apart or caring enough to save me when I was drowning. I forgive you for not hearing my pleas when my marriage was in shambles, but instead reminding me that Dalton was a good husband and I should ease up on him.

I forgive you for making me feel like a bad parent when you mocked and criticized my child-rearing skills and decisions. I forgive you for treating me like a child in front of my own children by undermining my authority in my own home and making me feel incompetent. I forgive you for your endless phone calls throughout the day to dictate every facet of my life. I forgive you for not loving me as I am and for who I am. I forgive you for teaching me to mask my pain, to cover up my hurt, and to never expose my truth. I learned what I lived, from your example. I forgive you for teaching me to silence my pain.

Although there were a total of 47 points of forgiveness made in my letter, nothing stands out more than me offering forgiveness to my mother for making me the glue to hold her and her marriage together, resulting in the burdens I had carried my entire life. As I wrote out each point of forgiveness, my heart wept and my eyes filled with tears, because in those experiences I needed saving, and no one came to my rescue. I was that little girl all over again boarding the bus to camp, being alone with a strange doctor, and getting between my parents when they were fighting. I was standing over my mom, trying to shake her back to consciousness, attempting to be my brother's guardian angel and keep him out of trouble. It was too much for a child to play such a grown up role.

My parents had a marriage that was typical of many households in the 1970's. The mothers were the primary caregivers, and the fathers did as they pleased, which often meant having several "girlfriends" outside of the marriage. We knew what my father was up to, but no one ever spoke a word about it, except when my parents fought. I often wondered why my mom wouldn't leave him. My dad has always been a selfish person, thinking only about his needs, wants and desires, and never considering the rest of his family. Despite her shortcomings, my mother did it all. She did her best to provide us with the greatest childhood she could manage.

    I saw my mom's struggles in her marriage, functioning like a single mother during most of my life. She was protective about some things, but naïve to most others, which is why I had so many issues with her. My dad was inconsiderate and unkind because my mom didn't matter to him. Well, that's the message we got loud and clear. Through his actions, my dad showed my brother and me that his family didn't matter. We were not a priority in his life, but we acted the part and pretended that everything was all right.

Chapter 36

When I finished writing the letter to my mom, it was time to reflect on forgiving my father. Gosh, there was so much to get out, and once I started writing I ended up with 135 points of forgiveness. It is not necessary to share all of them, but I am including the important ones, which helped shape me into the ball of confusion I had become.

Dad, I forgive you for not loving my mother enough and rendering her emotionally unavailable to parent Owen and me the way we needed her to. I forgive you for not supporting and encouraging my mother as a husband should. For believing that infidelity and dishonesty were acceptable, for having wandering eyes, and allowing yourself to be ruled by women. I forgive you for allowing my mother to act as if she was a single mother because you were absent from our lives. I forgive you for not investing the time required to nurture Owen and me to be well-balanced children and self-assured adults. For not loving us and making us feel like we didn't matter or were important. I forgive you for not respecting your family and the responsibility you had in leading your family. For using work as an excuse to be out of the house. I forgive you for dishonoring us and allowing others to use and abuse us in our own home. I forgive you for allowing your family from North Carolina to move into our home, displacing Owen and me from our private rooms to accommodate them. I forgive you for allowing your family to steal from us, especially the $2 bills Owen and I had spent so much time collecting. For teaching us that we are not worthy.

Dad, I forgive you for never expressing pride in our successes and for making me feel less than when you compared me to other people's accomplishments. I forgive you for the destruction you caused our family to suffer and never owning up to the chaos you forced us to endure. For living a double life where we were never the priority. I forgive you for parading around the four other children you fathered with another woman while you refused to spend quality time with Owen and me. Dad, I forgive you for giving your other children all of you, and leaving nothing for us. For allowing other women to disrespect my mother and our family, and not protecting us from such hatred. I forgive you for making me not trust you as my father, as you lied and manipulated our lives. I forgive you for never pouring value into me. For not being a leader of our family and demonstrating the role of a healthy man/father/husband relationship. For not demonstrating how to choose a spouse while staying true to my values or how to love and respect my husband. I forgive you for highlighting the most egregious qualities of relationships especially within a marriage. Dad, I forgive you for not showing me what true love looks like and feels like. For not protecting me when I needed my father the most.

Dad, I forgive you for making me tough when I wasn't. For making me assume responsibilities no child should have to take on. Dad, I forgive you for not seeing me, for allowing your fears to disrupt my life, and for not believing in me. For being selfish and never thinking about the welfare of your family's well-being. I forgive you for using me as a pawn in your life, as well as in your lies. Dad, I forgive you for forbidding me to be active in the church and doing what it took to have a relationship with God. Dad, I forgive you for showing my brother through your actions, deeds and words that he was never worthy of your love. I forgive you on behalf of my brother for allowing him to die without you making any attempts to heal his broken heart. I forgive you for never uttering the words "I love you" to Owen, or to any of us.

Nothing haunted me more than having to forgive my father for making me fill his shoes as husband, father, provider, protector, nurturer and other roles a family man is expected to perform, but he was too selfish to do. Moreover, I forgave my father for emotionally, mentally, and financially abusing my mother and treating her like dirt underneath his shoes. For lying, scheming, and doing everything within his power to show others that my mother meant nothing to him. I grudgingly forgave my father for making my mother so unhappy that she was emotionally unavailable to make me happy and for stealing my mother's joy and poisoning her soul with such toxic betrayal that lives within the deepest part of her being and will take a thousand lifetimes to heal.

"Don't hold your breath! Exhale. Inhale in. Exhale out. Inhale in, and let it out," I told myself.

Let it all flow out. Let it go. It's on paper now and out of you, the voice whispered. *Don't hold on to it anymore. Let it freely escape your grasp. You've been holding on for forty-four years. Let it go.*

Words that were never spoken and the impact of actions that cut ever so deeply were finally out in the open. With each point of forgiveness granted to my parents, I felt a little lighter.

The heaviness that had become an extension of me left my chest. I could breathe. Divorcing my parents proved to be the best part of the process because it gave me time to reflect and analyze the profound influence they both had on me, collectively and individually. They suffocated me with their own inadequacies, their fears, the generational curses and the blatant selfishness.

My brother and I were the recipients of the childhood my parents experienced with their own parents, their frustrations with each other, their lives and the world. Things their parents didn't give them as children had been extracted from us as well. Although my mother tried to do things differently, she was fighting against a force her passive self could never conquer. As a result, my brother and I were buried before we even had a chance to live. I'd held on to those experiences that contributed to my brokenness. Broken at the hands of my own parents, who should have molded and nurtured me and prepared me for the path I was to travel. Instead, they unknowingly placed roadblocks in the way, hurdles that should have never been positioned in my path in the first place. They knew they weren't perfect, but they had no idea every one of their actions had a crucial impact on my life. Because my parents didn't know better, they were unconcerned about doing better. It was time to break the cycle, and it started with me.

Chapter 37

I continued my weekly sessions with Dr. Benton and shared my forgiveness points with him. "Now it's time to confront them," he said.

"What? Wait, so I have to tell them what I've written?" I said.

"Yup!" he said causally.

"I can't!" I cried. "It will break their hearts to know how I feel. I can't show them the letters. They will be mad at me." I was afraid to share my feelings. I was already separated from my parents and even prevented them from contacting my children. Dalton was the only one speaking to my parents, and he assured them that I was ok. Apparently, they were worried about me, and the fact that they couldn't have any contact was as painful for them as it was for me. My mother questioned Dalton, constantly asking, "Who does this to their parents?" I wasn't sure I had it in me to confront my parents with the letters, fearing it would destroy our relationship and then I would definitely be divorced from them permanently. I didn't think I could sit in front of them and share what I had written. However, since this was part of the process, I had to find comfort in knowing that I was going to survive telling my parents the truth. This method was about authenticity and vulnerability, and sharing my truth with my parents was necessary.

As I engaged in my couch ministry month after month, and continued sessions with Dr. Benton every Monday, I started to understand the need to purge my thoughts. It felt good to write down my feelings regarding my parents' contribution in helping me build my walls of protection. With each sentence written, I started slowly removing the barrier, brick by brick. Nothing prepared me for the total breakdown I was about to encounter when I confronted Dalton with my true, unadulterated thoughts and feelings, which I had previously housed deep within me. Based on past experiences, I had shielded Dalton from my honesty, fearing he could never handle the truth. Reality stripped him of the protection he had created in his mind, as if the truth unleashed the security he needed for the lies he told himself. The truth, for Dalton, was like a free-fall into the unknown, and he would wildly attempt to grasp anything that secured him, even if what he grabbed had thorns that peeled away the skin on his hands.

Dalton and I had a meeting scheduled with the pastor of Dalton's childhood church, which I had been attending. We had been going to church regularly since returning from Turks and Caicos, and we felt called to do more within the church. During my healing process, Dalton and I had started to make significant efforts to repair our marriage. We read the Bible together, shared scriptures, and we were excited about inviting God into our union. We still had work to do, but we were in a much better place within ourselves and in our family dynamic than before we went to Turks and Caicos.

We wanted to meet with the pastor to share our healing journey, and to explore ways Dalton and I could use our experiences and backgrounds to become more connected to the body of Christ, the church. Relinquishing control to

Giving My Pain a Voice

Dalton the past few months had been extremely difficult for me, but definitely doable on most days. Therefore, Dalton was responsible for making the appointment and following up where needed.

All week we had been excited about our meeting. We had a 7:00 pm appointment on a Wednesday evening in December. We arrived ten minutes early and waited in the parking lot. 7:10 pm. 7:20 pm. No pastor. The office was dark, and there was no one in sight. "Did you follow up yesterday to confirm the appointment?" I asked.

"No, why would I? I made the appointment and the church secretary has my cell number, so if they needed to cancel they would have called," Dalton said.

"I always call the day before to confirm," I said.

"Well, I didn't," Dalton said. The longer we sat there, the angrier I became. Before we gave up and left the parking lot, Dalton called the church office, left a message and requested a call back. As we drove off, I remember feeling so irritated I could scream. We started arguing about the mishap and Dalton repeatedly said, "It's not my fault." I couldn't help but think that if I was in control and not letting Dalton "take care of me" I would have confirmed the appointment and we would have been sitting with the pastor right then.

The longer I stewed the more I hated being taken care of. It sounds crazy, but it's disappointing when people drop the ball and fail you, especially your husband. I was fuming, my lips were pursed tightly together and my heart was racing. On a scale of one to ten, I was at fifteen. *Ok, Anni, use your tools. What does this anger mean? What's it trying to tell me?* I contemplated the answers as we rode along in silence.

My thoughts were like a running argument. *I handle me better than anyone else handles me. But he made the appointment and did what he was supposed to do. Yeah, but if he called to confirm the day before, this would have never happened. Well, everyone makes mistakes. But this could have easily been avoided if he'd been responsible.* In the midst of my internal battle, Dalton drove to my in-laws' house and pulled into the driveway, but I had no idea why we were there. "Are you getting out?" Dalton asked.

"No!" I said sharply as he exited the car. I sat there and my anger turned to rage. Dalton returned ten minutes later. I kept quiet and said nothing during the remainder of the ride home, the rest of the night, or the next morning.

The following day, I got up and refused to let go of my anger. I wanted to hold on to it. Feel it. Let it fester within me. I was still livid about Dalton's irresponsibility and trying to process why it upset me so much. Regardless of who was at fault, my reaction had everything to do with me. It was about relinquishing control and being disappointed. It was how I felt about being taken care of, or *not* taken care of, as the case may be.

In a text sent to Dalton later that morning, I wrote, *In this moment, I feel no one (you, parents or friends) can take care of me better than me. I like my independence and the strength I have in it. Obviously, I know the devil is having his way with my thoughts, but I'm tired of fighting him. So, I'm angry, and I don't care.*

Afterward, I thought to myself, *What is my real issue with Dalton? Is it really the mishap with the appointment, or is it something bigger? Why do I expect him to be perfect?* I sat on the couch, but this time I didn't read the Bible or the daily devotional. I sat in silence to reflect on my relationship with Dalton, just as I had done with my parents.

He betrayed me! At one point in our relationship, I thought Dalton was perfect and took very good care of me, until he betrayed me, like my father betrayed my mother. He didn't care about being unfaithful, or hurting me, or making me feel guilty for wanting to leave him. He didn't care about my feelings at all. He, like others, failed me. Although my parents played a significant part in my troubled life, I don't think they held the starring role. Dalton played the lead character, and he stole the show by betraying me and breaking my heart. He was my knight in shining armor, but he never protected me. It turns out that I was the knight and he was the damsel in distress. He didn't rescue me and take care of me. I rescued him.

How could I relinquish my independence to a man who never took care of me or even knew how? I felt even more broken because of him. When I thought about it, I came to a stark realization. *It was not my parents who hurt me the most. Dalton has broken me.* Dalton had stripped me of who I was and allowed others to strip me as well. When he allowed his family to disrespect me, he left me vulnerable and alone, to fight my way through the tangled web of hurt, pain and rejection those women inflicted on me. I had every right to be angry! I was angry with Dalton! Agnes! Mrs. Johnson! Rachel! They treated me like garbage and tried to make me feel like I was not important, not worthy. They robbed me of my confidence, my good spirit, my dignity, and a bright vision for my future with Dalton and his son. All the while, Dalton stood by and watched it happen without saying a word. Yes, I was angry! In that moment of clarity, I began writing my forgiveness points to Dalton.

Chapter 38

There was a purpose in the pastor not showing up that night. That incident was the catalyst for writing down everything I held inside about Dalton and our relationship. I was shattered, but after all these years, I had yet to pick the pieces off the floor. My destiny was railroaded by Dalton, his family and my parents. My brother's death entangled the path, but Dalton was clearly the source. My parents contributed to my brokenness, yes, but I had managed to live with purpose, happiness, confidence and in truth of who I was until the first time Dalton betrayed me. That pivotal moment stirred up my past, and the wrong doings of my parents resurfaced.

I regretted allowing Dalton back into my life, as far back as our first year of dating. I hated what he had done to me. I blamed him for what he had *not* done, like refusing to stand up for me. I held Dalton responsible for the majority of the misery in my life, for my loss, my confusion, and my unhappiness. Every attempt I made to pull us together, he divided with his self-hatred and sabotage. I would fall back into the miserable routine, and Dalton helped pull me backward. He was killing me, emotionally and mentally, and I knew it.

My forgiveness points with Dalton brought up so much pain and hatred that my pen couldn't write fast enough. The hurt spilled out of my soul like a raging waterfall. My body grew hot and my face was flushed with the blood that was pumping overtime to keep up with my rapid heart rate. I went downstairs and knocked on the door to the guest bedroom where Dalton was watching TV. "Can I talk to you?" I asked with hesitation.

Dalton said, "Sure."

I walked into the room with my brown faux-leather journal in hand, and I said, "I have something I need to share with you."

He said, "Ok," but there was concern plastered on his face.

"Our meeting with Pastor Livingston didn't happen for a reason," I said. "That appointment not happening brought up a lot of anger in me, and I need to forgive you for the things I believe you have done." Dalton gave me a weary look, as if he was not prepared to hear anything I had to say. "Are you ok with me reading my forgiveness points to you?"

He sat up from the bed, took a deep breath, and put his right hand on his forehead, as if his head needed to be held up. "Yes," he finally said. Dalton fidgeted around on the bed until he found a comfortable position, and then took a deep breath.

"Dalton," I said. I looked into his eyes, and I felt my eyes fill with tears before I began reading. "I forgive you for cheating on me and waiting until three months before our wedding to tell me. For being a liar and deceitful. I forgive you for not believing I was good enough for you to remain faithful to me. For breaking up with me one year into our relationship. I forgive you for putting your friends and family ahead of me. For sucking the joy out of my life. I forgive you for making me live in the dark world you have occupied due to the complications of your life and adoption. I forgive you for making me solely responsible to keep you alive and fearful if I failed to do so. I forgive you for making me fall out of love with you because you didn't love yourself. For allowing your mother and family to treat me as if I was nothing. I forgive you for allowing Agnes, Rachel and Mrs. Johnson to put Christopher on a pedestal while treating our kids like they are not worthy of their attention."

I took a deep breath and continued. "I forgive you for not standing up for me and making me fight my own battles throughout our marriage. I forgive you for allowing Christopher's mother to control you, and for you compromising our relationship to please her. I forgive you for making me feel like a single parent because you were emotionally absent from our family. For guilting me into marrying you. I forgive you from stealing me away from myself. For not loving me the way I needed you to love me. For breaking my will and my drive to succeed. I forgive you for not protecting me. I forgive you for forcing me to be the leader of our family because you were incapable. For sabotaging everything I tried to make our family happy. For not standing strong in my time of weakness. I forgive you for not being the mature man I needed you to be when I was being sexually harassed at work."

"Dalton, I forgive you for not understanding the things I had to shoulder in this marriage. For making me feel guilty in my honesty because you couldn't handle the truth. I forgive you for not owning up to the damage you caused this family and especially to me. For not seeing how much I needed you, wanted you in my life. I forgive you for wasting my time and extinguishing my light, leaving me in the darkness to navigate myself and our kids through this life. I forgive you for destroying the excitement I once had about our future."

As I got to the next point, I started crying. I could barely get out the words as my voice trembled and my tears fell onto my journal, smearing some of the words. "Dalton," I said. I took a long deep breath in an attempt to pause for a moment.

"I forgive you for pulling a gun out and threatening to take your life, and possibly mine." I could barely clear my airway, and I felt like I was hyperventilating. The memory of those moments put me back in that space, and I remember how desperate I was to try to get Dalton to hear, see and smell my fear.

Dalton dropped his head in shame, and he did everything he could not to break down as I was struggling to finish. "I forgive you for not valuing me. For allowing your friends to disrespect me in front of you while you looked away. I forgive you for acting like I was the sole source of our problems. I forgive you for allowing your family to dictate how I could interact with Christopher. I forgive you for not staying true to the person you were the night I met you, the original person I fell in love with. I forgive you for pushing me away and making it hard to love you. I forgive you for making me afraid of you and not being able to tell you I was scared. I forgive you for not demonstrating the love you said you had for me. I forgive you for making our children wait every Christmas morning while you first went to your son's house to watch him open his gifts as soon as he woke up. In the meanwhile, our kids would wake up and have to sit and look at their gifts, waiting for you to return from the guilt trip Christopher's mother placed on you. I forgive you for putting Christopher and his mother first and causing our family to feel second best. I forgive you for making me sick from the stress I have carried. I forgive you for making love hurt."

The room was silent but filled with the enormous volume of each spoken word. As I sat sobbing, Dalton got up to retrieve tissues for me. "I'm sorry. I'm so sorry, Anni," Dalton said, with his shoulders hunched forward and his head hanging low. "I failed you. I failed us, and I'm truly sorry." I took a deep breath in and let out a tremendous exhale. I felt his genuineness. For the first time, I believed he got it! I was able to speak my truth in a fearless way. He was no monster.

He didn't intentionally want to hurt me. Dalton was broken himself. The weight of my words and his own suffering was evident as his body slumped down in resignation. "I'm sorry, babe," he said. "I ask for your forgiveness and God's mercy on me."

"Thank you, Dalton. I accept your apology," I said. We embraced, and I could tell that his strength was gone. He was a weakened man, but I refused to try to smooth it over. That's what I always did. Dalton needed to recognize the weight that had been sitting on me and come to terms with it. As we prepared for bed, my spirit was light and his was heavy.

Chapter 39

I shared my forgiveness points with Dr. Benton, and he was a bit shocked at how many I had regarding Dalton. He expressed feeling concern for Dalton, because that was a lot to handle, hearing that he was not a perfect man. In my discussion with Dr. Benton the 141 points of forgiveness for Dalton was actually linked to my father and his lack of protection, guidance, and healthy child-rearing, which caused me to pick a man just like him. I struggled with this notion, because I never viewed Dalton to be in the same category as my father, but in my heart, I knew there were some obvious similarities. I'd been indoctrinated by my parents to pick a man like Dalton.

I was groomed to care for broken people and accustomed to being dumped on by people who were supposed to love, nurture and care for me. Dalton fell within the lines of the cycle of dysfunction I was used to. My father destroyed our family with infidelity, lies, and selfishness, and robbed my mother of who she was designed to be. Therefore, generational patterns were being continued in my life, in my family and with my children. Carter and Alisa were living in an environment almost identical to what I'd lived as a child.

"Separate the bullets from the trigger," Dr. Benton would often say. "Your parents are the bullets and Dalton is the trigger. The bullets can't hurt you unless the trigger is pulled." The gun was loaded with bullets of pain, betrayal, hurt, and burdens from my parents, and Dalton pulled the trigger on all the issues. Dr. Benton confirmed my belief that God used the situation with Pastor Livingston not showing up to initiate a series of events intended to help me heal the wounds of my marriage and my past. The mishap over the appointment was in God's plan.

"God used a mistake to help you heal. God permits mistakes for our growth. God is in control," he said. Dr. Benton explained it so eloquently by saying, "When you have toxicity in your system, it must come out!" That's what forgiveness does. It sheds you of the pain and burdens that weigh down your soul. It's more about freeing yourself and no longer allowing the past to hold you in bondage. "Forgive yourself," Dr. Benton said. "Everyone needs forgiveness, including you."

The more I thought about forgiving myself, the more I could understand the importance of letting go of the thoughts I told myself all the time. We can be so hard on ourselves, with our own self-hate and negative talk. We contribute to our burdens and feelings of inadequacies by what we tell ourselves. *How could you be so stupid? Why do you always pick men like that? Why can't you be a perfect mother and show up to all the PTA functions and make homemade brownies? Why can't you be in ten places at one time? Why are you feeding your kids processed foods? Why isn't your house clean?*

We know those thoughts, right? I cannot be perfect and I will always make mistakes, but how I think has a direct impact on what I do. *Forgive yourself.*

Giving My Pain a Voice

I forgive myself for feeling like I have to be perfect. For deciding to marry Dalton, despite my gut telling me not to. I forgive myself for being convinced to do something I knew wasn't right for me and out of character. I forgive myself for marrying a man I did not trust. I forgive myself for giving up on me and losing my way. I forgive myself for not being truthful when I needed to be for my own sanity. For staying with a man I feared. I forgive myself for not sharing with my parents the hell I was living in my marriage. I forgive myself for believing my parents could save me. I forgive myself for failing in business and taking a job that I knew wasn't right for me. I forgive myself for picking a man like my father. I forgive myself for not doing anything sooner to save my children and myself. I forgive myself for dishonoring my own children by allowing the pathology of generations to influence my parenting. I forgive myself for telling myself I am not enough, that I'm not good enough, that I'm not worthy of the life I want, or capable to achieve my goals.

All that negativity needed to be buried once and for all. From now on, I had to be mindful of my thoughts and my perspective of how I viewed everything every day. My kids were watching, and I needed to set the example for them on what it means to be in relationship with God. How to forgive. How to grow and learn from mistakes of the past. How to be good to yourself. How to be patient. How to love. I was demonstrating these affirmations for my kids, as they witnessed me in my couch ministry, going to church, reading the Bible, sharing my relationship with God with them, showing what forgiveness looks like, and presenting a healthy marriage. They were the sponge, and I was the liquid. I allowed my children on this journey with me, because the things I was learning were important to teach them in order to break the cycle.

Writing down my hurt gave my pain a voice, and I felt ready to share my forgiveness points with my parents, as I had done with Dalton. Giving my pain a voice allowed me to express the magnitude of what they had done, and the impact they had on who I had become. They would see how they slowly buried me alive with their lack of compassion. They would have a visual of the generational patterns that had seeped into my life from theirs. Dalton could now understand how the darkness he carried all his life had no place in our marriage or in how we reared our children. My parents' and Dalton's backstories had been addressed to begin the process of ending the patterns of dysfunction that existed in our families.

Without coming to terms with your backstory, you'll forever walk amongst the crumbled bones of your existence.

I hadn't spoken to my parents in three months. When Dr. Benton suggested that I divorce them, I had been terrified. It was interesting to discover that I had found comfort in the process, and I easily recognized that they added a toxic mixture to my life. Removing them was like removing a gangrenous limb, painful but necessary in order for me to live and continue on my journey of self-discovery. My mind was clear and I didn't have anyone attempting to dictate my every decision or making me feel less than because my choices didn't agree with theirs. The separation from my parents was extraordinarily difficult. Nevertheless, like anything else, time heals.

It was time to meet with my parents and confront them with my points of forgiveness. This new age stuff was foreign to them, but they were willing to do whatever they must to get me back into their lives. Keep in mind, this was not going to be easy. There was no jotting down forgiveness points, sharing them with the ones to be forgiven, and then all was forgotten.

Boundaries must be maintained to prevent the toxicity from setting back in. Old habits die hard, but I had to stay the course to make sure my future relationship with my parents was going to be a healthy one. One that was respectful and honored the path that was leading me back to who I was designed to be and not who my parents cast me to be.

This process was teaching me that it was time for me to be selfish and create boundaries that were going to support me in establishing healthy and authentic relationships. My parents' response to our meeting was either going to be a positive step in the right direction or separate us forever. I had to be ok with either scenario.

Not everyone was going to understand my journey to healing, but I no longer cared because my survival was everything. There had been many attempts to kill my spirit at the hands of my own parents, my husband, and even some friends. I was at a point of strength, and I knew that every decision I made had to contribute to the health of my well-being.

Chapter 40

We set a date to meet with my parents and my therapist, Dr. Benton. In preparation, Dalton and I set the children down and explained the entire process to them, so they would know what to expect. Although the kids were not going to be a part of the session, we wanted to include them in the process as much as possible. My kids adored my parents. They were the only extended family members who had been present and active in their lives.

As we sat at the dining room table and began our discussion, my son became upset at the notion that I hadn't been speaking to my parents for three months. Because they had been busy with their own schedules, school assignments, friends and sports, they hadn't really noticed that we were not communicating.

Carter felt sorry for my mother and didn't think it was fair for me not to speak to her. "Grandma has it hard," he said as he began crying. "Why would you do that to her?" Fighting back tears myself, Dalton stepped in to explain the reason why I had stopped talking to my parents.

Alisa chimed in and said, "Sometimes people need space to figure things out." She could be so mature at times.

"It's still not fair," Carter responded and calmed down a bit.

"We're going to meet with them, and you'll see that grandma is fine," Dalton assured.

Carter wiped his tears and smiled at Alisa as she began to wiggle in her seat and sing, "We're gonna see Grandma and Grandpa and stay in the hotel, and we can bring our bathing suits, but I'm not getting my hair wet!"

"The hotel has a swimming pool?" Carter asked.

"Yup," Dalton said. That was the end of that conversation. I knew Carter was really upset and having a hard time understanding why I was not speaking to my mom, but at least the pool provided a distraction. Carter and Alisa ran off in excitement to search for their swim suits.

We had agreed that it would be best to meet in Dr. Benton's office in Maryland. It was a central location, and we were all staying at the same hotel as Dalton felt it was most convenient since the kids were with us. They were always super excited to see their grandparents, and this was no exception. I understood their enthusiasm as we drove to Maryland, but my purpose for the trip was to finally confront my parents and make more strides toward healing. I was ready but nervous.

Although I attempted to avoid my parents on the day of our arrival, I decided I should at least say hello before our meeting the next day. Carter and Alisa had already gone to their grandparents' room. Dalton escorted me to their room, and I was feeling anxious, taking deep breaths in and out, as we approached the door.

"You ready?" Dalton asked.

"I guess," I replied.

Dalton knocked on the hotel room door and I could hear the kids talking to their grandparents. Alisa opened the door, Dalton walked in, and I followed. Carter was talking to my father, who was seated at the desk. My dad, who was a bit hearing and visually impaired, kept talking to Carter because he didn't hear or see Dalton and me come in. My mother was standing between the two queen beds and turned around to face me as I walked in.

"Hello, hello, hello," I said as I walked past the bathroom.

My mom kept talking to Alisa, but she was looking at me, and I could tell right away that she was nervous and unsure what to say. I approached her, she held her arms open, and we embraced. I cried like a baby as my mother held me. This was the very first time I felt "seen" and emotionally acknowledged. She didn't pull away or push me aside. She held on, and in that moment I released all the forgiveness I had for her. With that embrace, and holding me while I cried, she gave me what I had been looking for all my life. A mother who was going to acknowledge me, my hurt, my pain, my fears, my insecurities and make me feel that everything was right with the world.

I was instantly lighter, and I knew that all would be forgiven. As my kids looked on, I realized this was the first time they had seen me really cry. To them, I was a pillar of strength, the one who fought everyone's battles, the person too brave to ever need anyone to save me and too independent to show my emotions. In that instant, with my mother's long awaited affection, I showed my children it was ok to be vulnerable. It was ok to cry. It was ok to be weak and allow someone to hold you up. I demonstrated how to forgive and what a daughter and mother relationship should look like. My mom and I let go of each other, and she said, "It's ok. I understand now. It's going to be ok."

I walked toward my father, who had been oblivious to my presence, and he said, "Hey! I didn't know that was you."

My encounter with my dad wasn't emotional at all. It was more matter of fact, but I could tell he was happy to see me as he stood to embrace me. We were a family of non-huggers, so his simple hug revealed his elation in seeing me. "You smell good, Toot," he said, using a nickname he liked to call me.

"You've lost weight," I said.

"Yeah, I haven't had much of an appetite lately, I guess," he said.

The kids watched the exchange as if they were watching a tennis match. Dalton told my parents that our meeting the next day was 10:30 am and that he would drive us there. I told my parents I would see them in the morning, and I left. Dalton and I started back to our room, and when we were in the elevator he asked, "How are you?"

"I feel good actually," I said. I was happy and less anxious about our meeting.

Chapter 41

We met in the lobby of the hotel, and my mother grabbed a few bananas from the breakfast buffet to take with her. As we gathered in the truck, I could see the nervousness on my mother's face. My father was calm and, to no one in particular, talked about the weather and the traffic they had encountered on their drive to Maryland.

When we exited the truck, I noticed my father's visual impairment seemed to be worse in the sunlight. He stumbled a few times, so I grabbed his arm to guide him along the way. Not wanting me to think he needed me to rescue him, he said, "I got it, Toot. I'm ok." To prove his point he jumped over one of the cement parking stops. We walked up the narrow staircase to Dr. Benton's office. I felt excited that it was almost time to let go of everything I'd held inside me for so long. I was no longer repeating the pathology of secrecy, holding everything inside and not letting anyone know how I was feeling.

We sat in the office waiting area, and my mother fumbled with the bananas on her lap while my father stretched his legs back and forth, bending them at the knee. Dr. Benton emerged from his office as another client was exiting.

"Hello," he said. This was the first time we'd met in person, and during the introduction he greeted everyone with a handshake.

Dalton was the only one with a serious look on his face. He liked to size people up before he decided if he wanted to engage in a conversation or not.

"Let's go, Mom. You're first up," Dr. Benton said with a friendly smile.

"Who, me?" Mom said with a surprised look on her face.

"Yes, you," I said jokingly.

Dr. Benton escorted my mother and me into his private office. After we sat down, he explained to my mother the process I'd been going through for the past three months and the purpose of the meeting. He said that nothing should be viewed as an attack, but counseled my mother to be receptive to the goals we were trying to accomplish. My mother sat attentive to every word Dr. Benton spoke as if she was a school-aged child being reprimanded for doing something bad.

"You ready?" he asked me.

"Yes," I replied.

"Let's go!" he said.

I turned to my mother, opened up my brown, well-worn journal and searched for the pages I wanted to share with her. I explained that I had written down things I believed she has done or allowed to be done to me in order for her to understand the impact her actions (or lack thereof) had caused me. The most important part was that I wanted to forgive her for the pain and suffering she had caused so we could move forward.

I began, and I started to cry as I struggled to get everything out. It was as if the pain was surging from my feet into my knees, my hips, stomach, ribs, and burning as it reached my throat. With every word spoken, I was being freed. Freed from my past. Freed from my mother's past and her mother's past. Freed from burdens of my mother's own childhood that had a direct impact on my childhood. Freed to be open to establishing a healthier mother/daughter relationship.

My mother was quiet and allowed me to get through each and every point of forgiveness I had written. When I finished, Dr. Benton turned to my mother and we both sat silently waiting for her to respond. "I'm sorry. I'm so sorry. I had no idea all this was going on, or that you felt this way," she said.

"You had no idea at all?" Dr. Benton asked. "No idea that you shouldn't leave your young daughter alone with a male doctor? No idea that your daughter needed your emotional support? No idea that your daughter should never have been used to hold your marriage together, or take on the adult responsibility of keeping a family intact?"

"No! I didn't know. I did the best I knew how. My mother left me when I was six months old. I was raised by my grandmother and my father. I gave my kids a better childhood than I had. I made sure of that," my mother said, defending herself. I felt like I needed to protect my mother, but I refused. I was no longer in the role of protector for my parents, so I sat back and watched the exchange.

I learned that in most cases, parents raise their kids how they were raised. My mother didn't know any better. She's a passive, naïve person who never fought for her own well-being. She stuck with my father, who emotionally and mentally abused her just as her father did. Generational patterns are real, but if you are not aware of those patterns, unfortunately they continue.

"I didn't know. I'm sorry I didn't know," she said in a frantic tone.

My mother could have benefited from therapy herself, because for the first time I saw a woman who carried a tremendous amount of unspoken pain. She acted it out unknowingly, but it was evident in her tone and in her aggressive behavior. Dr. Benton attempted to explore the impact of my grandmother's abandonment of her six children, but my mother was unable to dig that deep. "I was raised by my grandmother and she was my mother," my mother admitted. "I thought I had a good childhood. We didn't have any problems. I saw my mother one time in my life, when my daughter was eight years old. That's all I remember of her."

Dr. Benton ended the session with my mother by asking her to be open to seeking help in dealing with her backstory, so she too could heal from the suffering she was carrying. Although my mom did not acknowledge nor deny suffering, I could see how she was attempting to process everything that was being said. My mother was afraid.

"Do you have anything else to say to your mother?" Dr. Benton asked me.

"No. I put it all out there," I said with relief.

"I'm sorry. I'm really sorry, Anni," my mother said.

"I forgive you, Ma," I said with a smile on my face.

My mother struggled to get off the couch and asked Dr. Benton for help. "I'm an old woman, you know," she said, laughing as she stood to her feet. My mom was hilarious and loved to add humor to everything. It was comforting to see her joking with the doctor. As she walked through the threshold of the office doorway, she exhaled, looked at my father, and said, "Your turn."

Chapter 42

Before my dad entered the room, Dr. Benton asked if I needed a break, but I declined. I was ready! Dad entered the room with a different demeanor than my mother. He came into the room with a spring in his step, full of confidence. He seemed ready for a show down with the man responsible for advising his daughter to divorce her parents. Dr. Benton gave the same speech he gave my mother about the process of healing I had been in and the purpose of our meeting.

With my father's hearing impairment, he interrupted Dr. Benton several times with, "Say what again?" I reiterated what Dr. Benton was saying, to make certain he heard everything clearly.

Dr. Benton turned to me and said, "It's all on you."

I turned to my father, more determined and less emotional than with my mother. It was as if I didn't much care if I hurt his feelings. The majority of my points of forgiveness for my dad had already been shared with him over the years, through the confrontations and shouting matches we had had my entire life. My dad already knew the pain he had caused me, and I didn't believe there were going to be any surprise revelations made.

As I read aloud each point, he seemed unmoved and yet attentive to my words. I didn't cry or hesitate in my reading. I stopped occasionally to make sure he was hearing me clearly because I did not want him to miss something he couldn't hear. When I finished, my dad looked at Dr. Benton as if to say, "Ok?"

"Did you hear your daughter?" Dr. Benton asked.

"Yes, I did," Dad replied.

"Well?" Dr. Benton asked. I was surprised at how insightful Dad was in the explanation of his actions. He admitted that he was young and dumb and regretted many of the decisions he had made with his family, especially my mother. My dad knew his lack of respect and infidelity was not right, but he pointed out that he could not go back and change anything, although he wished he had the power to do so. Dad talked about being part of a dysfunctional family system, and at the time it wasn't considered unusual for fathers to stray from home while mothers tended to the children.

Dad talked about many regrets he had in his life, with the major one being his treatment of my brother, Owen. Dad said his lack of fatherly love toward my brother haunted him daily. My dad expressed realizing too late that his actions were detrimental to his first-born child, and he knew he was not a good role model or father to his son. He acknowledged that he made many mistakes in his life as a parent and spouse, and agreed to do his best at making amends.

My dad was a bit defensive and confrontational during the session, even challenging Dr. Benton to admit to being an imperfect father and husband himself. My father said he could never live up to the perfection of Jesus, but he said sternly that my relationship with him was definitely worth trying to fix, as he can see the impact his actions had on my life as a daughter, a mother, and a wife. My dad noted that men of his generation never shared anything. There was no going to a therapist to talk about emotions. "You learn by seeing," he said. "What your daddy do, you do. There was no heart-to-heart about right and wrong. There are curses that go from one generation to the next, and I'm cursed. I know it," he admitted.

My dad apologized to me and expressed his deepest sorrow in how he had contributed to the hole in my heart and the destruction of my mother's soul. I knew my father loved me. Unfortunately, it took me cutting him out of my life for him to appreciate me and gain a full understanding of the importance of making changes in his life, in his marriage, and with my family. "I love you with all my heart, and there is nothing in this world I wouldn't do for you. You have to know that," Dad said.

"I know," I said. As far as my mother was concerned, my dad knew he wasn't nice to her and treated her unfairly, but he hated being treated like a child, as if he was incompetent. He was aware of the damage he had caused her and the fact that he had turned her into such a resentful person that her pain was reflected in her hatred for him. He admitted choosing to deal with her wrath as his punishment, because she was who she was because of his mistreatment.

"Is there anything else you need to share with your father or ask him before we conclude?" Dr. Benton asked.

"No, I think everything has been laid on the line," I said.

Since there was nothing else to be said, Dad jumped up as if a needle had pierced his butt and said to Dr. Benton, "I hope to never see you again."

Dr. Benton quickly responded, "I hope not either." Dad strutted out of the office with his arms swinging side to side, walking like George Jefferson did on TV.

Chapter 43

The fear I had in sharing my innermost thoughts and feelings with my parents had disappeared. I was free, just like that. I felt lighter. It sounded crazy, but it was true. It was no longer about *them*. It no longer mattered how my parents felt. It was much more important about how *I* felt, regardless if they accepted what I had to say or not. I got what I had to say off my chest. The forgiveness was primarily for me, not them. I did not expect to go back to "business as usual." It was still important for me to maintain my boundaries with my parents and limit my phone conversations to once per week, with the possibility of more communication as time passed. I had to do what was healthy for me. No more toxicity was allowed in my life. I had to stay true to my boundaries and my overall healing and future health.

I sat in Dr. Benton's office after my dad left the room, assessing how I was feeling, and he called for Dalton to join us. From the moment I saw Dalton's face I could see that he appeared worried.

"How you feeling, man?" Dr. Benton asked Dalton causally.

"I'm good as long as Anni's good," Dalton said.

Dr. Benton acknowledged Dalton's strength in taking control of everything while I continued on my journey. Dr. Benton recognized the awesome responsibility Dalton had embraced to support me emotionally, mentally, physically, and financially. Just as Dr. Benton advised my mom, he stressed the importance of Dalton working on his own prayer life and seeking counseling to help him heal. Dalton nodded.

"You've been through a lot," Dr. Benton added. He explained to Dalton and me that self-discovery was vital for each person, but it also involved both parties who were committed to making the relationship work and thrive. One could not be alive and the other dead. The work came from both places and a healthy union could only be forged by both people entering the relationship as whole individuals.

"The work must continue on both ends of the spectrum," I added. Dalton nodded in agreement, but said very little.

"Is there anything you'd like to say to Dalton before we conclude our session?" Dr. Benton asked.

"Yes," I said.

I turned to Dalton and thanked him for his patience, understanding, and kindness throughout this process. I acknowledged how difficult the journey had been for our family, but especially for him, as he had to assume roles that were not yet comfortable for him. I thanked him for proving his ability to take care of me, and for supporting me in good and bad times. I thanked him for showing up when I needed him, and for seeing me, even when it caused him discomfort. I thanked him for loving me, despite my shortcomings, and welcomed him into my new life as we worked together toward healing our marriage.

"I love you," I said as I looked into his eyes so he could feel the sincerity and genuineness of my words.

"I love you too, babe," he said.

We both looked at Dr. Benton, and he said, "Ok! We're

done here, at least for today." Dr. Benton stressed that the work we put in to ourselves, our marriage, and our family had to continue beyond this session, and that we had to stay committed to infusing God in every corner of our lives. We needed to move forward on the path God had destined for us as individuals and collectively, as a family.

I continued my sessions with Dr. Benton every Monday to make certain I remained on a clear path and utilized the tools I had learned on the journey. I intended to work diligently to address obstacles, avoid negative thoughts, and be cognizant of generational patterns that would present themselves as I moved forward in my life, my marriage, my career, and as a mother to my children. I was committed to changing my life, breaking the cycle of dysfunction and pain, and accepting God's direction toward my destiny.

Since the time I had sat down with Dalton and read my forgiveness points to him, I had been concerned that his spirit was broken, as mine had been. In sharing this story, I have often portrayed him as the villain, but Dalton is not a bad person. Through this journey, I was able to look underneath the hurt he carried and see the strong, loving man I first fell in love with. Telling my truth has been difficult and it has forced Dalton to look at himself in a way he had always feared. It was time to take a good, authentic look in the mirror at the man he had become and find the man God meant him to be. He had done everything in his power to keep his emotions and feelings tightly secured and bottled up inside himself. They had been trying to escape since the revelation of his backstory emerged. How he had been conceived, his stay in foster care, his subsequent adoption, reuniting with his maternal and paternal birth family, and the life of secrecy that had unknowingly been passed down to him by his birth mother.

No more secrecy. No more hiding. It was time to shake up the bottle and watch the carbonated bubbles of his hidden agony race to the top, burst from its tightly kept container, and let his truth explode.

Perhaps one day I'll be able to share Dalton's journey with you. Dalton's adoption produced insecurities and he suffered as a result of the circumstances of being given up by his birth mother, and then being treated as less than by his adoptive family due to their dysfunction. It created a man that was wounded and needed healing. His story will provide insights into the emotional path he walked, alone and with me as his crutch.

When Dalton is able to process the pain from his backstory, he will be freed from those burdens. I anxiously await the unveiling of that man, his presence, his mind, body, and soul, the man God chose solely for me.

Epilogue

My Process to Healing

Although I've been extremely candid and descriptive in documenting my story, I want to add some additional information about my process in order to assist anyone who is contemplating a similar journey. I know how difficult it is to live with pain, suffering, loss, dysfunction, and other heavy burdens. I offer these thoughts and suggestions along with my prayer that God will direct your path toward wholeness and healing.

Make Time for God and Listen to His Instructions

God requires our undivided attention. He needs us to sit still and be quiet. This is a difficult task for most people, as we tend to think about our to-do list or have other fleeting thoughts running in and out of our mind. We do everything possible to distract ourselves, because simply put, quiet time is difficult. As you've read in my story, I had a tough time with my couch ministry. I did everything possible *not* to sit on that couch. My mind tried to convince me not to waste time on the couch.

I complained to Dr. Benton about sitting on the couch, about how stupid it was, and how unproductive I felt. Over time, I realized the importance of my couch ministry. I needed to share my day with God while He helped me work things out and gain a better perspective on the decisions I had to make. I brought my confusion to God on that couch. I stayed committed to sitting there because that was the only way I was going to be successful in solidifying my relationship with God. You have to give God his time.

I used the time to familiarize myself with the Bible by reading scriptures. I'm not well versed in the Bible and I still have trouble finding certain books as I flip through it. I reviewed Sunday sermons, devotional books, and Bible study notes. I did anything to gain an understanding of who God was, what He wanted from me, and how He will help me through life. I talked to God as I would talk to someone standing in front of me. I prayed and asked questions about things I didn't understand. On some days, I yelled at God when I was frustrated or angry with Him. I cried when I was sad, confused, mad, overwhelmed and when I felt lost. I treated God like my best friend. I shared every thought and emotion with Him from my seat on my couch. This routine takes time to develop, and you have to force yourself to stay committed to what God requires of you. You don't have to sit there all day like I did. Begin with a half hour in the morning before you start your day, and a half hour before you retire to bed. This is the first step in moving you closer to the life you want.

Of course, you can speak to God anywhere and at any time, but it was important for me to have a scheduled time every day where God and I would converse with one another. He used our time wisely by taking the opportunity of my stillness to instruct or direct me on my path. God would show up in scripture, sermons and sometimes through other people, who would surprisingly bring up a specific situation I was dealing with, and offer sound advice.

It took a while for me to hear God. Discerning between my own voice in my head and His voice was extremely difficult, and I still struggle with that. The more I sat on the couch, the clearer His voice became. The less time I spent on the couch, the more ambiguous His voice was. When I was far away from God, it was nearly impossible for me to hear His directions for my life. God needs to have you close to Him. He wants to share with you, guide you, and direct you to the life He has preselected for you. He's not able to do that if you do not dedicate time specifically for Him, and condition yourself to listen. His voice is soft, like a whisper. He'll tell you things that sometimes don't make sense or scare you absolutely to death. Just like when He told me to quit my job. He was right, because He has been blessing me with pay increases on every career opportunity I've had since then, even the offer to name my own salary.

Be Humble

God will make you feel convicted over decisions you've made that don't sit well with Him by causing you to wrestle with sleepless nights or a nagging feeling you can't escape. For example, I had an argument with my neighbor, who I had accused of ignoring my son on his way to the bus stop one morning. I was mad that she hadn't offered him a ride. I sent her a nasty text message and vowed never to ever speak to her again. The same night I tossed and turned. The next morning, I sat on the couch feeling uneasy the entire day. The voice said, *Fix it.* I ignored the voice, because I wasn't going to apologize after the mean things I'd written in the text. Besides, the friendship never felt right, and this was the straw that broke the camel's back. For a second night, I tossed and turned.

The next morning, I had gone to get my hair done, and on my way home, the voice said, *If her car is there, you must apologize.* I knew it was a weekday and she should be at work, so I was confident that her car would not be there. However, I turned the corner onto my block, and there it was, her car sitting in her driveway. I pulled in to my driveway in disbelief and refused to go. *You have to make this right, and you have to do it now!* the voice rang in my head. "Ugh," I said, as I put my car in reverse and backed out of my driveway. I pulled up to her house and hesitated. *I'm sure she's not there. I'll ring the bell anyway, and leave after a few seconds if no one answers the door.* I walked up the driveway to the front door, rang the bell and waited. As I was about to turn away, the door opened. My heart dropped and I was standing in the face of humility as she motioned with her hand for me to come in. I tucked my tail and openly began to apologize as tears filled my eyes and fell down my face. God knew she would accept my apology and lined up everything for me to experience what it felt like to be vulnerable, authentic, and humble. God speaks all the time. You must have the courage to act on what he tells you, even if it scares you. It's a test of your courage and trust in Him.

Down in the Belly of the Pit

The pit is a dark place. Not too many people have the courage to visit, let alone hang around and sift through the remains. Most folks avoid going there like the plague, for fear of what might surface as things are stirred up. The pit is for the brave at heart. The ones who are scared to death, but go anyway. They are determined to lift the veil of truth, courageously walk on red-hot coals, and demonstrate the daring it takes to visit such a dismal place, and the strength it takes to heal. Whether you're healing from an abusive past, emotional turmoil, or a life-altering setback, a pit visit is necessary. You must dredge up the unresolved matter that keeps you in bondage and purge those elements that no longer serve a purpose in your life.

Unforgiveness usually settles into the foundation of your pit. It anchors you to your life. There are some bones in the pit that are more scarred than others. Some have layers of patches over holes that have been drilled there at the hands of someone else. Sometimes empty promises can be seen in the pit, as shattered pieces of glass that are stained by the glue used to piece them together. There is a lot of hurt and pain in most people's pits. The intertwining vines of resentment that link the bones together securely fasten them to the foundation of unforgiveness and create a tormented soul. Unfortunately, the people who have come and gone in our lives have left their marks on our souls, both good and bad. You can't leave the stain of pain, hurt and resentment untouched if you wish to embrace the life God has ordered for you prior to your physical birth.

God continues to heal me, provided I have the courage to take this journey. It was not easy as I faced my own truths and promises that had been shattered, which contributed in shaping me into the woman I had become. Tyrese's song resonated to my spirit, because I needed to address the imprint of pain that had been left behind by my parents, Dalton, and others in my life. I needed forgiveness. I needed to lift the shame. I needed a change in my life. I needed my parents and my husband to empathize, witness and experience the hurt they had caused me and ask for my forgiveness. More importantly, I needed to look at the truth for what is was and forgive them.

The Father, the Son, and the Holy Spirit are there every step of the way as you navigate through your pit. They help you uncover those things that need revealing to enable you to move forward. They are there through the pain, hurt and sorrow that are kicked around while you explore. They hold you up and support you through the process, and carry you when you are too tired to continue. One thing is for sure, when you're down there in the pit, the Holy Trinity will not leave you nor forsake you. Keep your focus on God, openly communicate, and seek professional help as you embark on your journey. Get involved in a church and be a part of the Body of Christ, and stay true to God's will for your life.

Have Faith

Hebrews 11:1 (KJV) says, "Faith is the substance of things hoped for, the evidence of things not seen." As I mentioned in my story, this was the only Bible verse I could recite from heart. I learned it in Sunday school from Brother Troy at my Aunt Ruth's church. Being a visual person, I always had a hard time imagining what it meant to have faith. You often hear folks quote the scripture, "If you have faith as small as a mustard seed...nothing will be impossible for you." (Matthew 17:20 NIV.) Well, a mustard seed is extremely tiny, and before I began my journey, I'm not sure I had even that much faith.

I had difficulty understanding the expression, "Let go and let God." I learned a great lesson in what it means during a recent visit to North Carolina during spring break with my son. Carter and I had flown down for a five-day visit to my parents' house while my daughter was on a ten day European trip with her school. This was the first time I had been there since I started my healing process. With my dad's visual impairment, I wanted to spend my time giving my mother a break from having to drive my father everywhere. My dad was, and still is, an active business owner. He hates staying still, and spends most of his days running around, bidding on jobs for his lucrative trucking business, checking the status of jobs in progress, or meeting with people interested in his services.

"Come on and take a ride with me, Toot," he said.

My mom gave me a funny look and chuckled as she said, "You'd better take some snacks with you." We left the house, and bucked our seatbelts when we got settled in the car.

"Go down there to the end of the dirt road and make a right," Dad directed.

"Ok," I replied as I put the car in reverse and backed out of the dirt and grass covered driveway. I made the right turn as instructed. "Where are we going?" I asked.

"We're going down here," he said ambiguously as he answered numerous work related calls. I passed a few intersections. In between his calls, I asked, "When do I have to turn?"

"Drive straight," he said.

"How many lights down do I have to go?" I asked again.

"Go straight, please," he said again, as if I hadn't heard him the first time. I drove straight, as instructed, but I was getting frustrated about not knowing where I was going or which way I needed to turn. The voice said, *Sit back and relax.* The more calls my father took, the more frustrated I became. The voice, a bit more insistently said, *Enjoy the ride. I'll let you know when you need to turn.*

I took a deep breath and kept driving straight as instructed, no longer distracted with Dad's phone calls. I turned up the radio slightly and slowed my pace. *That's right. Stay in the moment. Take each mile as it comes,* the voice reminded me. I was at peace as I let go of the need to know where I was going, how long before I had to turn, or the time left to get to the destination. My dad looked up and said, "Turn left at the next light, Toot." I turned left and continued driving until my dad gave me the next instruction. The need to know where I was going no longer mattered.

That's what faith looks and feels like. God will give you enough notice when it's time to change directions. Stop looking to be miles ahead when you haven't even gotten through the first few miles. Everything happens in God's time, no matter how much we want to speed up the process. I'm no expert at this faith thing. I still struggle (figuratively) that I have faith to be in sunny California…you know, "things hoped for"… but somehow, I'm still in New York. Keep the faith, and God will work out the rest.

Surrender

Surrendering to God's will and not my own was a battle of strength and control. I thought I could strong-arm God because I was successful and had managed without Him for over forty-four years. I had orchestrated my life according to my own will and accomplished everything based on the responsibility that had been bestowed upon me by my parents. I took control over Dalton's life and became the nurturer he needed and wanted. I managed the unnatural order of my household as I wore the pants that were meant for Dalton to wear.

I believed I did it all until I was faced with that immovable brick wall. My strength and determination was unable to chisel away at the wall that stood in between the life I was living and the life I was destined to live. That wall was a permanent structure that I had no ability to tear down, climb over, or build a doorway to go through. I didn't have anything that would enable me to pass the obstacle blocking my way. God made it clear that the only way to conquer the wall was to depend on Him. God wanted the opportunity to take care of me. To eliminate my fear and frustration. To nurture me and allow Him to carry me. God wanted me to abandon my futile efforts to challenge the wall, give up the fight, and realize I would never break down the wall without Him. He wanted me to surrender. Not by waving a little white flag. He wanted me to close my eyes and free-fall into His open arms, and trust Him enough to believe He would catch me. He wanted me to be weightless and allow my body to dangle like a rag-doll.

You see, God has a plan. He needs to be in control of your life, to move you around freely without any tension or attempts to push back. He wants to mold you into who He needs you to be. He needs to use you for His purpose without you trying to pull away. He wants to control you without you trying to manipulate, calculate, or second-guess His decisions.

I learned I am no match for God. I had tried it my way for most of my life, and although He has allowed me to travel on my manmade road, He put obstacles in my path that only He could move. He drew me in and enveloped me when I finally gave up fighting. Getting close to God is necessary; it's only difficult if you resist. He can't direct you if you won't allow him. Give yourself permission to lie lifeless in His arms. Deny the urge to take control. Accept the blessings He has in store for your life, and watch the wonders unfold.

Surrendering requires consciousness, and you'll find the necessity to submit to God's will numerous times each day. We are creatures of habit, and it's easy to fall back into our old ways and fail to yield to God's way. Be mindful of your actions daily, and live moment by moment to ensure God's will is the most important thing in your life.

Trust the Process

The process of healing takes courage, patience, and perseverance. It challenges you to face your fears head on. The process makes you feel as if you're going crazy and sometimes physically sick. It drains you of every ounce of energy you have in your body and still expects you to rise above it. It beats you down into the ground, smashes your face in the gravel and leaves you with visible scars for everyone to see. The progression leaves you lost in the middle of a 750 acre wooded property at night, and you are expected to emerge unscathed. This forest contains every phobia you have and all the unspeakable fears you dare not share with anyone. Can you hear God over the pounding beat of your fearful heart as you are lost in unfamiliar territory?

In times like these, when we're afraid and unsure what to do, isn't God the first person we call to for help? You can either stand still and hope that someone comes to rescue you, or you can start praying and asking God to begin to direct your steps towards finding a way out the wilderness. Step by step, God reveals a solution. Inch by inch, you move closer to discovering your way. Trusting God through adversity, believing He will make your path straight and your vision clear, is the full embodiment of what it means to trust the process.

Staying committed and trusting the process isn't always pretty, neat or exciting. Nevertheless, it is a true testament of your strength and determination. Dedication is required in order for you to live the life God has planned. God captures and arrests us to move us toward His vision for our life. The story of Job describes it best. Job had everything taken away from him, but he stayed true to God, and he refused to denounce Him. Job emerged victorious when God blessed him abundantly, with more than what had been lost. Despite the odds, or what it may look or feel like, God wants you to stay true to your relationship with Him as He continuously works behind the scenes of your life.

Although my testimony is not as dramatic as Job's, God placed that brick wall in my life to awaken me to the life he had always envisioned. God's plan is always so much bigger and vast than anything we could ever visualize for ourselves. I was so focused on growing my business that I couldn't see God had a different plan. Every attempt I made to get it off the ground, God intervened. I tried every avenue possible, including selling my integrity and my happiness for money. God knew I was unable to bring direction to someone else's life if I didn't have order in my own. God needed to get me back to the default mode in which he created me. A reset, if you will. God needed to reboot me to a time in my life where my innocence sparked my curiosity to explore the world in a vulnerable and authentic state of being. A world where fear was not a factor and the influences of others hadn't began to take shape. A world full of endless possibilities where I believed I could accomplish whatever dreams captured my heart.

This healing process proved to me that, with God, the universe, or whatever you refer to as your higher power, as the captain of your soul, the impossible is always possible. As I look back on my journey and see how far I've come, I am excited about where God will lead me. He has placed new ideas and dreams within me and has broadened my vision to include things I had never imagined at the start of my journey. I remain committed to the ongoing life process each day, and I'm reminded daily to weave God's word, instructions, teachings, and presence into my life, my marriage, and my parenting. I thank Him for everything He brings in and out of my life, including people who teach me lessons, and those I can teach. I am enough, just as I am, to do God's work and live out my purpose in helping others.

Acknowledgments

First, I'd like to give all the glory, honor and praise to Almighty God for being patient with me throughout the many mistakes I've made and still showing me mercy and kindness in leading me toward discovering my purpose in this life.

I'd like to thank my husband for his courage in supporting me through my spiritual warfare and holding firm to the love he has for me despite his own personal pain and the burdens he struggles to face. The strength of our love can only be a testament to God's wisdom in knowing He placed us two together for His divine purpose. As we move forward as a three-stranded cord, I'm excited about the plans He has for us and what we can accomplish in our lives as well as in the lives of others as we share our experiences.

I'd like to thank my children for their patience and love throughout my journey. It pains me that I unknowingly allowed generational patterns and dysfunction to enter our family and our home. I promise to live more consciously and be a better mother, so they too can enjoy the life they were meant to live. I want to thank my parents for being open to such an unorthodox process of allowing me to verbalize my hurt while staying receptive to my feelings and loving me anyway. I'm grateful for their love and support, and giving my brother and me the best of what they knew how to give. I look forward to embracing a healthier and more authentic relationship. I want to thank my brother, who occupies a special corner of my heart, for showing me how to live unafraid.

In addition to my family's support, many people were instrumental in helping me in my life and during the writing of this book. My best friends, Kameron and Emily, continue to be sounding boards and trusted confidants. My girl, Denise, for pulling my coattail when my fear attempts to jump in the driver's seat. Raya, my dot sister, was an inspiration and champion in urging me to seek the help I needed. Dr. Benton, for teaching me to stand firm in my confidence and know that I am worthy and enough because God's got my back! My godmother, Emma for always telling me to take it one day at a time and never get ahead of myself. Lila and Michael for helping Dalton and me make our house a home with their interior design ideas.

I thank all the people that have added value to my life, in addition to those who have taken away. You have each made me stronger and wiser. I'm thankful for the lessons learned. I don't personally know celebrities like Oprah Winfrey, Gayle King, or Lucy Kaylin but they have made a huge impact on my process to healing. Thank you for helping me connect the dots of my experiences. Miraval Resort provided a vehicle to help me recognize my fears and tackle them head on.

Last, but certainly not least, a big thanks to Susan Barnes, a fellow Virgo, who totally understands my perfectionism and tendency to over analyze and assisted me in fine-tuning my thoughts. Thank you for delicately handling my story. I could not have gotten through the process of writing this book without you.

Resources

Shame - Songwriters: SAM DEES, RON KERSEY, TYRESE DARNELL GIBSON, WARREN CAMPBELL, DEWAYNE JULIUS SR. ROGERS © Peermusic Publishing, Warner/Chappell Music, Inc., Universal Music Publishing Group. For non-commercial use only. https://en.wikipedia.org/wiki/Shame_(Tyrese_song)

http://www.annibjohnson.com

Bible verses have been verified through https://www.biblegateway.com/

Faith is the substance of things hoped for, the evidence of things not seen. Hebrews 11:1 KJV

For the love of money is the root of all evil. 1 Timothy 6:10 KJV

But those who hope in the Lord will renew their strength. They will soar on wings like eagles; they will run and not grow weary, they will walk and not be faint. Isaiah 40:31 NIV

Serve one another humbly in love. For the entire law is fulfilled in keeping this one command: "Love your neighbor as yourself." Galatians 5:13-14 NIV

I will put breath in you, and you will come to life. Ezekiel 37:6 NIV

I will put my Spirit in you and you will live. Ezekiel 37:14 NIV

I am going to open your graves and bring you up from them. Ezekiel 37:12 NIV

So do not fear, for I am with you; do not be dismayed, for I am your God. I will strengthen you and help you; I will uphold you with my righteous right hand. Isaiah 41:10 NIV

For truly I tell you, if you have faith the size of a mustard seed... nothing will be impossible for you. Matthew 17:20 NIV

About the Author

Anni B. Johnson has successfully fused her education, professional experiences, and personal stories to create a platform to empower healthy and authentic relationships.

As she embarked on her journey, Anni began a quest to discover the life God intended for her to live. She had a calling to share her story, and she accomplished this by writing her first book, *Giving My Pain a Voice: A Path to Healing*. Anni is passionate about her mission and is led to move forward with additional writing projects, speaking engagements, and life coaching. Her gift and her goals in life are to help others recognize the process of recovery from dysfunction, teach people how they too can overcome adversity, and live the life God has intended for them.

Anni is a native New Yorker who enjoys being in community with others, sharing love and laughter, and traveling with family and friends, which always includes a location with "blue water." Anni stays busy with her family and her career, but she finds time to read, indulge her love of good food, and enjoy nature walks, which always provide peace and clarity.

For additional information, conference, workshop or vendor opportunities please visit www.annibjohnson.com.

www.ingramcontent.com/pod-product-compliance
Lightning Source LLC
Chambersburg PA
CBHW032107090426
42743CB00007B/262